THE WARS OF
EDUARD SHEVARDNADZE

THE WARS OF
EDUARD
SHEVARDNADZE

Carolyn McGiffert Ekedahl
and
Melvin A. Goodman

The Pennsylvania State University Press
University Park, Pennsylvania

Library of Congress Cataloging-in-Publication Data

Ekedahl, Carolyn McGiffert.
     The wars of Eduard Shevardnadze / Carolyn McGiffert Ekedahl and
Melvin A. Goodman.

          p.   cm.
     Includes bibliographical references and index.
     ISBN 0-271-01604-3 (alk. paper)
     1. Shevardnadze, Eduard Amvrosievich.   2. Statesmen—Soviet Union—
Biography.   3. Soviet Union—Foreign relations—1985–1991.
I. Goodman, Melvin A. (Melvin Allan), 1938– .   II. Title.
DK290.3.S54E38   1997
947.085'4'092—dc20
     [B]   96–19615
                                                                                              CIP

It is the policy of The Pennsylvania State University Press to use acid-free paper for
the first printing of all clothbound books. Publications on uncoated stock satisfy the
minimum requirements of American National Standard for Information Sciences—
Permanence of Paper for Printed Library Materials, ANSI Z39.48—1992.

The views expressed herein are those of the authors and not those of the U.S.
government.

We dedicate this book to the memory of

Lenore Goodman Stein
and
James B. McGiffert

for their unfailing love and encouragement

Contents

Preface   xi

Introduction   xv

Map of the Commonwealth of Independent States—
  European States   xxiv

Map of Georgia   xxv

Prologue   3

1. SHEVARDNADZE'S ROOTS:
  THE SEEDS OF REFORM   7

    Modest Beginnings
    Early Career
    Moscow Connections
    Reformer and Innovator
    The Negative Legacy of Repression
    Retrospective

2. EVOLUTION OF A POLITICAL PARTNERSHIP   29

    Early Friendship
    One Man's Choice
    Foreign Ministry Years, 1985–1990
    The Rift Between Gorbachev and Shevardnadze
    Retrospective

3. DOMESTIC IMPERATIVE:
  THE NEED TO REFORM   51

    Out of Isolation Toward a New World Order
    Economic and Political Inheritance
    International Legacy
    Domestic Links to Foreign Policy
    Axioms of New Political Thinking
    New Assumptions

4. ROCKING THE BOAT:
SHEVARDNADZE BATTLES THE BUREAUCRACY   71
   Rebuilding the Foreign Ministry
   Taking on the Military
   Minimizing the Party's Role

5. THE CENTRALITY OF THE UNITED STATES   100
   The Reagan Administration
   The Bush Administration
   Shevardnadze's Legacy

6. MOSCOW'S CONSCIENCE ON HUMAN RIGHTS   130
   Human Rights Legacy
   Viewing the World "Through the Eyes of Humanity"
   The Turn
   Moscow's Conscience on Human Rights
   Washington Drags Its Heels
   Shevardnadze's Impact

7. NEW DIRECTIONS IN EUROPE   152
   Perestroika and Policy Toward Europe
   The Liberation of Eastern Europe
   The Last Straw: Reunification of Germany
   Shevardnadze and the Diplomacy of Reunification
   The Compromise
   European Legacy

8. RETREAT FROM THE THIRD WORLD:
OUT OF AFGHANISTAN INTO THE GULF WAR   183
   Retreat from Afghanistan
   The Persian Gulf War

9. APPROACH TO THIRD WORLD TENSIONS:
FROM EXPLOITATION TO RESOLUTION   206
   Inheritance: A Cold War Perspective
   Shevardnadze's View of the Third World
   Rapprochement in Asia
   Toward Peace in the Middle East
   Withdrawal from Africa
   Letting Go in Central America
   Shevardnadze's Legacy

10. SHEVARDNADZE'S RESIGNATION:
THE END OF THE ROAD   237
   The Resignation
   Prologue to Parting

Reaction to the Resignation
Repercussions of the Resignation
The Coup

11. ABROAD AT HOME   257
The Russian Bear Roams the Caucasus
The Irony of Shevardnadze's Return
Georgian Nationalism
Shevardnadze Makes a Deal with the Devil
The Failure of the U.S. Connection
The Impact of Chechnya on The Caucasus
The Problems of Crime and Corruption
Shevardnadze's Fate

Epilogue   285

Notes   291

Selected Bibliography   319

Index   325

Preface

Two years before Mikhail Gorbachev's accession to power in 1985, Georgetown University sponsored an intense eighteen-month effort by thirty-five experts and scholars to study the Soviet Union. Two years after his accession, the Rand Corporation sponsored a book entitled *The Future of the Soviet Empire*, which focused on Moscow's impressive capabilities for expansion and aggression. Neither study provided clues to the strange death of Soviet communism less than ten years later. Both reiterated much of the mythology about the Soviet empire that led the West to miss signs of its coming collapse; they attributed to the Soviet Union the second largest economy in the world—a typical mistake on the part of the Western scholars. At the same time, many observers argued that the United States was in decline and lacked the will to check Soviet military power. When the Soviet Union finally collapsed in 1991, however, the same observers concluded that Western policy was somehow responsible for its destabilization.

Gorbachev and his foreign minister, Eduard Shevardnadze, did not share the belief that the Soviet Union was the world's second strongest economic power, nor did they believe the United States was in decline. They knew the Soviet Union was desperately weak economically, that its defense burden threatened to overwhelm it, and that it had made a series of foreign policy blunders that had cost it dearly. On a beach at Pitsunda, a resort on the Black Sea in Georgia, Shevardnadze told Gorbachev in 1984, "Everything's rotten," and the two men agreed that they couldn't go on like this. *Perestroika* and *glasnost* were born out of this profound dissatisfaction with the Soviet Union's situation, broadly shared by most of the Soviet Union's elite. Only seven years after this conversation, the Soviet Union had ceased to exist and Russia had become just another troubled state trying to make the difficult transition to democracy and a market economy.

In this book, we describe and analyze Shevardnadze's contribution to the effort to restructure Soviet domestic policy and revolutionize foreign policy. We also assess his responsibility for the Soviet collapse and the leadership role he played in the independent state of Georgia that emerged after the collapse. Shevardnadze was a committed advocate of fundamental systemic change. He knew that Moscow had devoted far too many resources to the interests of the Red Army, and he understood that a stable relationship with the United States was critical if reform were to succeed. He also realized that the Soviet Union must become a construc- tive, nonthreatening member of the international community if it were to gain access to the credits and technology necessary for competition in the global economy. His willingness to act decisively on these assump- tions made him the moral force of "new thinking" and the point man for the policies of perestroika.

Shevardnadze was a product of the Soviet system that he sought to change and that he ultimately would help to destroy. He was a skillful politician who exploited the available instruments of power to advance his career and further his policy objectives. He ruthlessly repressed dissidents and removed both real and potential opponents. As Georgian party leader, he acted the role of ultimate sycophant to the leaders of the Soviet Union, outrageously extolling the virtues of those who were in a position to help him.

As longtime analysts of the Soviet system, we were intrigued by the role Shevardnadze played in the radical redefining of Soviet foreign policy that began in 1985. We watched as he and Gorbachev rejected fundamental Soviet assumptions and reversed long-standing policies in an effort to end the U.S.-Soviet rivalry that had cost both countries so much. We were impressed by Shevardnadze's commitment to reform, demonstrated by his dramatic resignation in December 1990, as well as by his political prescience, revealed in his warning of the right-wing coup that actually occurred eight months later.

As the history of the end of the Cold War began to be written in the West, however, we were struck by the fact that Shevardnadze's role was barely mentioned. Articles and reminiscences focused on the endemic weaknesses of the Soviet system and the steadfast policies of the West, and failed to credit the Soviet leaders who had seen the need for reform and had undertaken policies designed to accomplish profound but peaceful change. We decided to cooperate in an effort to tell Shevardnadze's story.

As we embarked on the project, we realized we had access to a number of former Soviet and U.S. officials who had participated in the events we were exploring. We began by interviewing those individuals we actually knew, then expanded our efforts when we understood the wealth of information and insight we could gain from the process. In the course of interviewing and researching, we learned a great deal about Shevardnadze and had to adjust the story accordingly.

When we began, our overwhelming image of Shevardnadze was that of a hero who had played a critical and largely unheralded role in ending the Cold War. While we continue to view him as a heroic figure in that sense, we have also come to see him as a far more complicated and ambiguous figure—a ruthless political infighter capable of taking whatever action he considered necessary to further his own objectives. We cannot yet make a final judgment about the man and his contribution, but we believe he deserves attention as a major figure in the end of the Cold War, and we hope that this book will help focus attention on him and his partners in perestroika, Mikhail Gorbachev and Alexander Yakovlev.

We have received assistance from many people in writing this book, although they have no responsibility for either the results or our conclusions. Ambassador Victor Israelyan, a veteran of more than thirty years in the Soviet foreign ministry, was particularly generous with his time and energy, offering us his unique insights and introducing us to the fragmented and fractious world of politics in Georgia. While he himself was treated unfairly by Shevardnadze, he kept his personal experiences and feelings to himself until after our project was completed. He remained scholarly and objective throughout our meetings with him, and his analysis of Shevardnadze's personality and the impact he had on foreign policy decision-making and an entire generation of Soviet policymakers was extremely helpful to us.

Former secretaries of state George P. Shultz and James A. Baker III made time available for lengthy interviews, presumably because of their deep and abiding respect for Shevardnadze. Richard Schifter provided important testimony to Shevardnadze's recognition of the vital link between Soviet-American relations and human rights issues. Ambassador Jack F. Matlock Jr. provided insights from his experiences at the National Security Council and Spaso House in Moscow.

Shevardnadze's closest aide, Sergey Tarasenko, and Mikhail Gorbachev's interpreter, Pavel Palazchenko, were candid in their observations about the relationship between Gorbachev and Shevardnadze and brought a scholarly perspective to Soviet-American relations and the end of the Cold War. With the help of David Chikvaidze, we were able to meet and interview Shevardnadze during his visit to Washington, D.C., in 1994. We interviewed some forty American, Russian, and Georgian officials for this book, and we are grateful to all of them for their generous contributions of time and memory.

Several other individuals were a particular source of encouragement for this project. Our thanks go to Dr. Robert H. Ferrell of Indiana University, who once again interrupted his own schedule to encourage and guide the efforts of a former student. Major General John Fryer (ret.), former commandant of the National War College, is that rare soldier who understands the importance of scholarship to the college's teaching faculty and was willing to endorse a research sabbatical at a crucial phase in the project. Ambassador David Newsom and Hans Binnendijk of Georgetown University's Institute for the Study of Diplomacy provided space and support during early stages of research and drafting. Peter J. Potter and Peggy Hoover of The Pennsylvania State University Press were patient and helpful in handling a manuscript that took longer to write than initially planned.

We are particularly grateful to our children—Craig, Suzy, Kristen, Michael, Jonathan, and David—for their constant encouragement and support for us and for a project that often seemed as if it would never end.

Introduction

Assessing the impact of the individual on history is one of the most difficult challenges in political analysis. We know that the actions of individual leaders make a difference, but the relative importance of their actions, when set against broad social, economic, and political trends, is difficult to establish. Woodrow Wilson, Franklin Delano Roosevelt, and Winston Churchill changed the course of twentieth-century history in significant and easily identifiable ways. Recognizing the role of a great contemporary leader in determining the course of history is more difficult; we lack sufficient perspective on the period, and the consequences of specific actions remain unclear.[1]

We have tended to underestimate the role played by the last leaders of the Soviet Union, because historians have focused on the societal problems that precipitated that country's collapse and because political commentators have engaged in protracted debate about the contribution Western policies made. The ultimate dissolution of the Soviet empire may have been inevitable, and the policies of the West undoubtedly had an impact, but the actions Soviet leaders took determined the timing and the nature of the collapse. Peaceful change was possible only because those who came to power in Moscow in 1985 were committed to domestic reform, to reconciliation with the West, and to the nonuse of force.

Just as the Russian Revolution of October 1917 as defined by Lenin influenced the course of modern history, the Soviet revolution as defined by Mikhail Gorbachev, Eduard Shevardnadze, and Alexander Yakovlev is having a profound impact on contemporary history. Their readiness to halt the arms race, to renounce political and military dominance over Eastern Europe, and to retreat from the Third World ended the superpower competition that had defined the post–World War II era. Their policies precipitated peaceful anticommunist revolutions in Eastern Europe and redefined the international system. By stabilizing the USSR's external position, Soviet leaders prepared their nation for its virtually nonviolent collapse.

Historians speculate about what the consequences would have been *if* General Robert E. Lee had won at Gettysburg or *if* Hitler had decided not to wage war on two fronts. We can ask, *What if* Gorbachev, Shevardnadze, and Yakovlev had not been the stewards of Kremlin policy in the 1980s? Without these unusual leaders, it is unlikely that the Soviet Union would have pursued a policy of deliberate and peaceful retreat. With different leaders, Moscow might have opposed the liberation of Eastern Europe and the reunification of Germany. There would have been no immediate end to the Cold War, and the arms race would have continued to drain resources in both the East and the West. Conflict resolution in the Middle East, Africa, Central America, and Southeast Asia still would be constrained by superpower competition, and the war in the Persian Gulf might have been more protracted, if it had been waged at all.

Without enlightened leadership, the decline of the Soviet Union would have continued, but at a slower pace and in a far more dangerous manner. Defiance in Eastern Europe might have provoked military intervention, as occurred decades earlier in East Germany, Hungary, and Czechoslovakia. Different Soviet leaders might not have "kept the troops in the barracks" at times of crisis, such as the collapse of the Berlin Wall in 1989. They might have responded to dissatisfaction at home by creating problems abroad, exacerbating relations with the United States and provoking tension in the Third World.

Shevardnadze played a critical role in conceptualizing and implementing the Soviet Union's dramatic about-face in the 1980s, which ended the Cold War and created a completely new international environment. Considered the moral force for "new thinking," he was the point man in the struggle to undermine the forces of inertia at home and end Moscow's isolation abroad. Both Secretaries of State George Shultz and James Baker have credited Shevardnadze with convincing them that Moscow was committed to serious negotiations. Each became a proponent of reconciliation in administrations that were intensely anti-Soviet. They concluded that the history of Soviet-American relations and the end of the Cold War would have been far different if it were not for the personal diplomacy of Eduard Shevardnadze.

Gorbachev, Shevardnadze, and Yakovlev came to power convinced that the Soviet system was in severe decline. They recognized that the most serious problem was economic and that revitalizing the economy superseded any possible military threat. As they wrestled with possible solutions to the economic crisis, they realized that foreign policy would have to change profoundly if they were to succeed at home. Gorbachev and Yakovlev focused on domestic reform, and Shevardnadze took the lead in redirecting foreign policy to create an international environment conducive to reform. At the heart of their approach was the understanding that the security of the Soviet Union could best be served by improving relations with the West. A more relaxed international environment and an easing of the crushing military burden through arms control agreements would permit a refocusing of resources on domestic problems.

Shevardnadze understood that it was necessary to reject the ideological assumptions that had produced a costly arms competition, a series of foreign policy blunders, and Moscow's isolation from the international community. He believed that the Soviet Union must become a normal member of the international community if it were to share in the benefits of global economic development. He directed his energies to improving Moscow's relations with the United States and to ending the arms race, promoting international stability and gaining access to Western loans, investment, and technology.

The new Soviet leaders certainly did not anticipate the enormous impact their policies would have on the international system—that they would in fact precipitate the collapse of the postwar order. Their fundamental motive for pursuing domestic reform was to preserve socialism, and their motive for making radical changes in foreign policy was to redefine but strengthen Moscow's position in the international system. Their strategy was logical and pragmatic, but it was also inherently radical and ultimately destabilizing.

The major theme that runs throughout this book is the wars that Shevardnadze fought at home and abroad. His major domestic battle was with the military, which had tremendous status and wielded inordinate influence over foreign policy decision-making. He believed that economic revival demanded major reductions in the military budget and that, to achieve this end, Soviet society must be demilitarized and the military monopoly in formulating national security policy broken. Doing so required dispelling many assumptions about the military and challenging the viability of former policies, thereby undercutting the military's legitimacy. Shevardnadze's commentary on these subjects formed a comprehensive critique of military decision-making since the end of World War II.[2] Exploiting the military's failure to achieve victory in Afghanistan, he challenged the value of intervention abroad, attacked the defense budget, and fought for arms control agreements and unilateral force reductions.

Shevardnadze also waged a campaign against communist ideology as a basis for formulating foreign policy. In an extraordinary speech to the Ministry of Foreign Affairs in July 1988, he asserted that there was no longer any connection between foreign policy and the class struggle, thus becoming the first Soviet spokesman to formalize explicitly the de-ideologization of Soviet foreign policy.[3] This speech and its line carried the day, but it exacerbated Shevardnadze's relations with party conservatives who later would join the military in seeking his downfall.

Ultimately, Shevardnadze struggled with his partner in perestroika, Mikhail Gorbachev. As their policies precipitated radical changes and drew increasing criticism, they reacted in different ways. Gorbachev equivocated; he sought to slow the pace of reform and pacify the military, and increasingly he followed the advice of Shevardnadze's critics. Shevardnadze, convinced that the old order could not be preserved, became committed to radical change. Eventually he parted company with Gorbachev, resigning in December 1990 because his old ally had failed to support his policies and defend him against harsh criticism. In his resignation speech, Shevardnadze provided a dramatic and, as it turned out, prescient warning that the Soviet Union was slipping back toward repression, dictatorship, and the use of force.

Shevardnadze also had his foreign battles to fight. Moscow's international position in 1985 was no more promising than its domestic situation. U.S.-Soviet arms control talks were nonexistent, and U.S. ideological opposition to dealing with the Soviet Union had reached its apex; Eastern Europe had become a significant burden on the Soviet Union, and Soviet prospects were in decline in Western Europe; Soviet relations with China were strained, and the Soviet position in the Third World was stagnant. The Soviet Union had become a status quo power, sustaining some of the more repressive and impoverished regimes in the world. Since the Bolshevik Revolution, Moscow's approach to the international system had been shaped by competition with the West, commitment to expanding the world socialist system, and isolation from the global economy. Shevardnadze realized that these assumptions had to change and that he would have to convince domestic and foreign antagonists that fundamental change was necessary and genuine.

Shevardnadze understood that in order to change the Soviet Union's international position it was necessary to alter the "atmosphere prevailing over our contacts with the nations that are most important in deciding the political climate of our planet."[4] His immediate focus therefore was on improving relations with the United States. During his first two years as foreign minister, Shevardnadze offered concessions on issues that he believed would have resonance in Washington, making one gesture after another in his efforts to forge a new relationship. His support for deep reductions in the Soviet arsenal eventually led to disarmament agreements that were overwhelmingly favorable to the United States, allowing Washington to get "120 percent of what it wanted" in negotiations with the Kremlin, according to U.S. Ambassador Jack Matlock.[5]

Shevardnadze also pressed for radical change in Soviet policy on humanitarian issues, believing that a more enlightened approach would lead to closer Soviet-American relations and increased Western economic and technical assistance. He moved to end repression against dissidents and refuseniks, forcing this policy on reluctant leaders at home. Shevardnadze was responsible for ending the quota system for Soviet Jewish emigration, which had been a major obstacle to improved U.S.-Soviet relations since the 1970s. In 1985, fewer than 1,000 Soviet Jews were permitted to leave the country annually; the number of Jewish emigrés exceeded 70,000 by 1989, and virtually free emigration was in effect by the time he resigned.

Shevardnadze failed to reap the anticipated benefits of his concessions because of Washington's disbelief and skepticism. The United States, which had spent so much treasure countering the Soviet threat, failed to see how decrepit the Soviet Union had become and how great an opportunity was being offered. President Ronald Reagan saw the struggle between the United States and the USSR as one between good and evil until Secretary of State Shultz finally persuaded him that he could reach historic agreements with the Soviets.[6] President George Bush came to office believing that Shultz had been too eager to improve bilateral relations, but Secretary of State Baker eventually came to believe that Moscow was genuinely committed to redefining relations and persuaded the president to continue negotiations with Moscow. Each administration lost valuable time that could have been well spent in efforts to stabilize

Moscow's strategic arsenal and anchor Moscow to the international community.

Because the United States was so slow to respond and offered so little in return for major Soviet concessions, Shevardnadze faced severe criticism at home. He was attacked for making unilateral force reductions and granting the United States one-sided agreements. Through it all, Washington pushed Shevardnadze as far as possible in negotiations, rather than protecting him from his domestic opposition. Ironically, his greatest success—establishing close working relations with Washington and helping to end the Cold War—would become one of the major reasons for his downfall.

Shevardnadze also understood that Moscow had to change its relations with Europe. Strategic arms agreements with the United States captured the headlines, but the real savings in the defense budget were to be found in conventional arms agreements and unilateral reductions in Eastern Europe, where the Soviets maintained a costly military presence. Shevardnadze argued for greater political sovereignty in Eastern Europe, which meant ending the Brezhnev Doctrine, which proclaimed Moscow's right to intervene to defend communist regimes and enforced Eastern Europe's submission to Moscow. The retreat from Eastern Europe—the most dramatic shift in Soviet policy since the end of World War II—led to anticommunist revolutions in Eastern Europe in 1989 and an end to the Soviet military threat to Western Europe.

Moscow's decision to accede to the reunification of Germany further contributed to profound changes on the Continent. In this case, while not the creator of policy, Shevardnadze played a key role by accepting what had become an inevitability and by taking on the task of convincing opponents at home. He had no grand design for resolving the German problem and no particular interest in German reunification; he and Gorbachev did not prepare themselves—let alone their colleagues and constituents—for the political and psychological impact of reunification. The notion of a reunified Germany as a member of NATO was particular heresy and provoked strong opposition in Moscow. At the 28th (and last) Soviet Communist Party Congress in July 1990, Shevardnadze was severely criticized for "totally destroying" the Warsaw Pact, the "camp of socialism as a whole," and the party's ideology.[7]

Recognizing that Moscow's aggressive policies in the Third World had damaged relations with the United States, Shevardnadze began a retreat from the Third World. The formal decision to withdraw from Afghanistan predated Shevardnadze's appointment as foreign minister, but he became the chief architect of its implementation and accomplished his objective by acquiescing to virtually every demand the United States made. The Soviets agreed in 1988 to withdraw their troops from Afghanistan within ten months no matter what the situation on the ground might be and without any guarantees for the safety of the Najibullah government. Withdrawal began in May and, by February 1989, in spite of the ongoing insurgent challenge to the Kabul regime, Soviet ground troops had been withdrawn.

Shevardnadze was solely responsible for the unprecedented cooperation between the United States and the Soviet Union during the crisis in the Persian Gulf in 1990–91.[8] In pursuing his U.S.-centered policy, he had to overcome strong domestic opposition and numerous differences with Washington. Moscow's support for U.S. policy was critical to the success of Desert Storm and Desert Shield, and Shevardnadze was the driving force behind that support. It would have been a "very difficult history" without Shevardnadze, according to National Security Adviser Brent Scowcroft.[9] Without Moscow's retreat from Central Europe, Washington's transfer of most of its forces and armor in Europe to the Gulf would have been far more hazardous, if not impossible.

Many high-ranking Soviet diplomats and military officials believed Shevardnadze's approach was wrong and conveyed their views to Gorbachev, who agreed to send Yevgeny Primakov as a special emissary to Saddam Hussein in October 1990. Primakov, a frequent critic of Shevardnadze's policies in 1990, would succeed Andrey Kozyrev as Russian foreign minister in 1996. Having lost a major policy debate, Shevardnadze thought seriously about resigning in October 1990.[10] He decided against it, however, and maintained his policy of support for U.S. action.

Shevardnadze ultimately lost his battle in Moscow. He and Gorbachev failed to create effective institutions to replace those they undermined, largely because of their authoritarian style. Increasingly, they relied on their own views rather than on consultation either within existing institutions or outside. The collapse of perestroika, symbolized by Gorbachev's move to the right, forced Shevardnadze's resignation in 1990. The collapse of the decision-making system in the Soviet Union, demonstrated by the attempted coup against Gorbachev in August 1991, produced the disintegration of the Soviet Union in December.

Shevardnadze later criticized himself for rushing the transition from totalitarianism to democracy and sponsoring a revolution from above. "We tried to create a new reality by the old methods, sending out directives from above," he conceded. A "few people got together and decided that they couldn't go on like this, but when they tried to figure out how they could go on, they disagreed."[11] He acknowledged that he had underestimated the political and social forces opposed to change.

In 1992, Shevardnadze returned to an independent Georgia in far worse shape than when he had left nearly seven years earlier. Civil strife was destroying the country, and the economy was in ruins. He was forced to pursue a humiliating course, taking Georgia into the Russian-dominated Commonwealth of Independent States and requesting a Russian military presence in western Georgia to counter secessionist forces in Abkhazia. Just as he had been accused of selling out to Western interests when he was foreign minister, Shevardnadze was charged with betraying Georgian interests as chairman of his ancestral homeland.

It is one of the great ironies of this period that independence for Georgia brought Shevardnadze, the radical reformer, back to Tbilisi in the familiar role of unelected autocrat. As party leader in Georgia in the 1970s and early 1980s, he had battled corruption and introduced the most liberal political and economic reforms of any Soviet regional leader. In the late 1980s, he pushed strenuously for radical reform in the Soviet Union. When he returned to Georgia, however, he ruled by emergency decree, without the legitimacy of law and with the support of corrupt and brutal paramilitary forces. Finally, elected Georgia's second president in 1995, he embarked on another campaign to rid Georgia of corruption, reform the economy, and restore political stability.

The man who placed the Soviet Union on the path of dramatic reform and resigned in protest over Gorbachev's drifting from that course thus became the authoritarian leader of the weakest republic of the fragmented superpower. The master politician again adapted quickly. He had lost none of the skills he had mastered as a republic party leader, including the ability to overcome his opponents, brutally if necessary. His career appeared to have come full circle.

Shevardnadze's personality helped him frame and implement the policies he espoused. He was neither political philosopher nor master strategist, but rather a superb politician—opportunistic, flexible, pragmatic, and ruthless. He was not a diplomat, immersed in the complexities of international discourse and hesitant to act; he was a man of action, a problem-solver impatient with obstacles—and a brutal infighter. As foreign minister, Shevardnadze drew his political legitimacy from his closeness to Gorbachev rather than from the Communist Party. His confident assumption that he had the Soviet leader's imprimatur to effect change gave him far more credibility and authority than any previous foreign minister. Finally, unlike his predecessors, Shevardnadze was not Russian, and he lacked the typical Russian distrust of the West. He was a Georgian, given to innovative thinking and bold actions.

Our purpose is to explain Shevardnadze's role in the revolution of Soviet foreign policy and the disintegration of the Soviet Union and its empire. This is a book about the accomplishments of a great man, a man of profound contradictions, whose story has not yet been told and whose contributions have been overlooked. We will deal with the kind of man he was and why he could do what he did, focusing on his accomplishments, the tensions in his personality and policies, his shortcomings and failures.

Our goal is to shed light on a number of puzzling questions. How did this "Soviet man" become an exponent of radical reform? What was the division of labor between Shevardnadze and Gorbachev? What caused their split in 1990? What legacy did Shevardnadze leave, and what was his responsibility for the dissolution of the Soviet Union? Why did Shevardnadze inspire such opposition and hostility not only in Moscow but also in Tbilisi, which was remarkably inhospitable to the most famous Georgian since Stalin? Finally, what was Shevardnadze's role in post-Soviet Georgia, and do Russian-Georgian relations provide clues to the fate of the Commonwealth of Independent States and Russia's potential efforts to restore its empire?

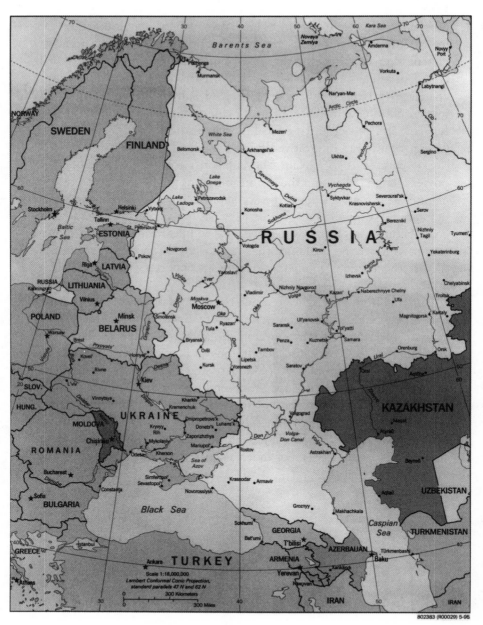

Commonwealth of Independent States — European States

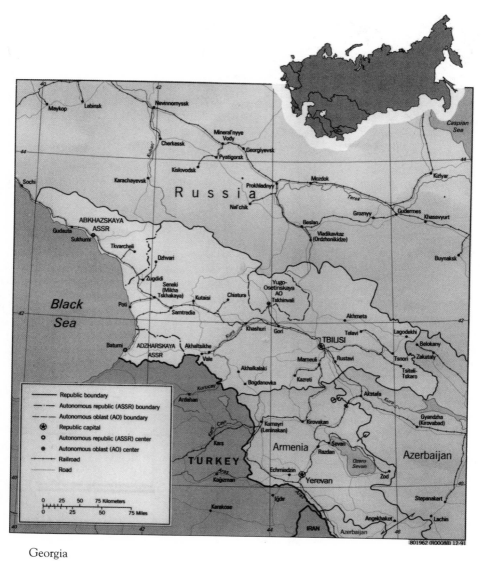

Georgia

THE WARS OF
EDUARD
SHEVARDNADZE

Prologue

Early in the afternoon of August 29, 1995, President Eduard Shevardnadze received a dramatic reminder that his nation was only a heartbeat from anarchy. As he left the parliament and headed for a party celebrating Georgia's new constitution, a large bomb exploded near his car. With only slightly better timing, it would have killed the Georgian leader and sent the country into another round of turmoil. Instead of toasting his nation's progress toward democracy, Shevardnadze found himself in the hospital, dazed and bloody though not seriously hurt.

There were many plausible suspects and potential scapegoats for the assassination attempt. Shevardnadze had earned many enemies during his numerous battles at home and abroad over the previous three decades and had survived other attempts on his life. Since his return home in 1992, Georgia had experienced two separatist wars and a civil war. Shevardnadze also carried the legacy of his own tortuous relationship with Russia, where he was blamed for the collapse of the Soviet Union; Ambassador Anatoly Dobrynin's memoirs even suggest that Shevardnadze anticipated the Soviet collapse, Georgian independence, and his return to Tbilisi as head of state.[1]

As a result, at the top of the list of suspected assassins in 1995 were the Russians, particularly the military, who blamed Shevardnadze for the demise of the Warsaw Pact and the deterioration of the Red Army. Russia fostered instability in Georgia to weaken Shevardnadze and to regain influence and presence in the Caucasus. In the summer of 1995, Shevardnadze's successful efforts to gain international support for the rebuilding of an energy pipeline from oil-rich Azerbaijan to Georgia's Black Sea coast particularly angered Moscow. Russian leaders were determined that oil should flow north through Russia. Consequently, they may have decided to remind Georgia of its vulnerability.[2] The detonation of the bomb only three days before Turkish Prime Minister Tansu Ciller's visit to Tbilisi also could have been designed to send a signal to Turkey, which had offered to fund the Georgian route. At his joint press conference with Ciller, when asked if he thought the assassination attempt might have been related to the pipeline dispute, Shevardnadze exclaimed,"Now you are asking the right question!"[3] In the time-honored tradition of blaming Moscow for most things that go wrong in Tbilisi, one of Shevardnadze's friends responded to a question about the possible perpetrators of the assassination by saying, "The answer, I think, lies to the north."[4]

Speculation about a possible Russian role in the assassination attempt was fueled by the fact that another suspect, the head of the Georgian security service, Igor Giorgadze, had made an unofficial visit to Moscow immediately before the attack. The Kremlin's subsequent refusal to extradite him further incriminated Moscow. Igor's father, Panteleimon Giorgadze, the leader of the Georgian Communist Party, was a longtime critic of Shevardnadze; Giorgadze's deputy, Temur Khachishzili, arrested three weeks after the attack, was the most senior Georgian official arrested in connection with the car bombing.

There were other suspects in the assassination attempt against Shevardnadze. Khachishzili had close ties to Jaba Ioseliani's Mkhedrioni, once the strongest and most independent paramilitary organization in Georgia. These groups fostered violence and corruption within Georgia, and their presence remained strong in Tbilisi, where the most fashionable men strutted the boulevards in black leather jackets and dark aviator sunglasses, carrying revolvers in Italian handbags. By the summer of 1995, Shevardnadze had begun to move against the paramilitary units.

Ioseliani, one of the most flamboyant figures in modern Georgian history, was a convicted bankrobber, and also a famous playwright and political dissident. He was part of the ruling troika that had ousted Georgian President Zviad Gamsakhurdia and invited Shevardnadze to return to Georgia in 1992. However, Ioseliani had become a political rival of the president, and several weeks before the assassination attempt he accused Shevardnadze of making Georgia a "Soviet state . . . a police state."[5]

Shevardnadze, who had been making serious efforts to disarm Ioseliani's paramilitary organization, used the attack as a pretext to move against his former ally. He had the police seal Ioseliani's parliament offices, where they reportedly found a cache of weapons and ammunition. Ioseliani's parliamentary immunity was removed and he was arrested—the warrant issued only one day after the car bomb exploded.[6]

The supporters of Shevardnadze's predecessor, Zviad Gamsakhurdia, the first elected president of Georgia, also were high on the list of possible assassins, and the Georgian police immediately began to round up active "Zviadists." The Gamsakhurdia and Shevardnadze families had been political rivals for generations, and the two men themselves had been bitter political opponents for two decades. Gamsakhurdia's security forces reportedly had tried to execute Ioseliani in 1992 for his role in the ouster of the president, using a device similar to that used in the Shevardnadze assassination attempt.

Finally, there was an "Abkhazian trail" that possibly led to the attack. In 1993, in an effort to end a struggle with Abkhazian separatists, Shevardnadze traveled to the beleaguered Black Sea resort of Sukhumi in Abkhazia, where Georgian forces waged an inept resistance to rebels backed by a small Russian force. Shevardnadze, displaying typical courage and braggadocio, refused to be evacuated, claiming he would stay until the end; he finally left the city only hours before the separatists captured it. Shevardnadze's continued vows to regain Abkhazia may have inspired an Abkhazian reprisal.

The actual culprits may never be identified, but in the wake of the assassination attempt Shevardnadze became a safer man and Tbilisi became a safer place. The president acquired an armored Mercedes-Benz limousine from the German government for his own use, but, more important, he moved rapidly and ruthlessly against his opponents. Ioseliani, both a suspect and a serious antagonist, was in jail, and his paramilitary organization was largely disarmed. Giorgadze remained in Moscow as repeated Georgian attempts to have him extradited to Tbilisi were rejected. Hundreds of political opponents, both real and imagined, were arrested. The communists went back underground, radical nationalists went into hiding, and in December 1995 Shevardnadze disbanded an elite security force that may have been implicated in the assassination attempt.[7]

Georgia had faced more than its share of anarchy following the collapse of the Soviet Union in December 1991. Gamsakhurdia had used his overwhelming electoral victory to arrest political opponents in Tbilisi and subdue the South Ossetians in the northern part of the country. He alienated most of his closest political supporters, including Prime Minister Tengiz Sigua and Defense Minister Tengiz Kitovani, and virtually the entire country was in revolt. Gamsakhurdia's opponents quickly formed a military council, surrounded the parliament building, where he had taken refuge, and eventually seized power. The president fled the country—first to Armenia and then to the breakaway Russian province of Chechnya in the North Caucasus.

If Shevardnadze had been killed in 1995, Georgia's international standing would have been compromised and the ethnic separatist movements in Abkhazia and South Ossetia emboldened. The separatists would have found it easier to justify their demands to secede from Georgia, and the Tbilisi government would have been politically paralyzed. A palace coup, perhaps with the support of the Russian Federation, would have led to the reappearance of various paramilitary organizations, particularly Ioseliani's Mkhedrioni. Chaos would have dominated the country once again.

Shevardnadze, a brilliant and ruthless political infighter, is steeped in the twelfth-century writings of the Georgian author Shota Rustaveli, whose epic poem "The Knight in the Panther's Skin" extolled the virtues of the free life of a Caucasian mountaineer and his heroic death. Educated Georgians can recite Rustaveli from memory, and Georgian brides were once required to know selections of his poetry for the entertainment of their husbands. Casting himself in the role of a courageous and bold Rustaveli hero, Shevardnadze took on the challenge of bringing stability to his ancient and romantic nation. Success in this venture would enable him to go down in history as the father of the modern Georgian state as well as the statesman who played a major role in ending the Cold War between the United States and the Soviet Union.

1

SHEVARDNADZE'S ROOTS

The Seeds of Reform

> The rules of the game made no provision for any exception. . . . There was just one way out—not taking part.
>
> —Eduard Shevardnadze

Eduard Shevardnadze's roots are in Georgia, where he was both autocratic Communist Party leader (condemned for obeisance to Moscow and brutal repression) and innovative reformer (praised for efforts to end corruption, energize the economy, and expand political dialogue). His life and career before 1985 were spent in Georgia, and it is there that one must look for the clues to his becoming the driving force of the second Soviet revolution and the implementer of "new political thinking" in Soviet foreign policy.

Shevardnadze's career in Georgia was filled with contradictions. His climb to the top of the Communist Party displayed ambitious careerism and crass opportunism. As party leader and security minister, he played the role of loyalist, paying homage to the Soviet system and its leaders and ruthlessly suppressing dissent and nationalism. He was responsible for the arrest, torture, and execution of thousands of extortionists and black-marketeers, as well as numerous dissidents and Georgian nationalists. He demonstrated his ability to tack with the political winds and do whatever was necessary to satisfy his personal ambition and achieve his political objectives.

It was also during his career in Georgia that Shevardnadze displayed the unusual courage, initiative, and pragmatism that revealed his potential as a reformer. His ability to embrace radical ideas was unusual in a Soviet leader and suggests that he was more committed to practical results than to ideology. His doubts about the Soviet system began in the 1950s, when First Secretary Nikita Khrushchev denounced the excesses of the Stalinist era. These doubts intensified over the years until he finally agreed with Mikhail Gorbachev that the whole system was rotten.

As party leader in Georgia, Shevardnadze operated in unique and unorthodox ways, confident in his own judgment and committed to pursuing the course that would best serve his interests and advance his goals. He cultivated powerful patrons in Moscow and manipulated the system skillfully. At the same time, he pursued policies that, in the Soviet context, were liberal and enlightened. He made full use of his position and power in true autocratic fashion, but he also appreciated and used sophisticated political tactics, such as cultivating the support and cooperation of the general public. In short, Shevardnadze was an extraordinarily skilled, resilient, and ambitious politician who demonstrated during his Georgian career that he was capable of both ruthless careerism and political creativity.

MODEST BEGINNINGS

Eduard Shevardnadze was born on January 28, 1928, in the tiny village of Mamati in Georgia's Guria Province. His father, Ambrose, who taught Russian language and literature in the village school, was a member of the Communist Party and frequently argued politics with his brother and brother-in-law. As a boy, Shevardnadze found it difficult to take sides during these arguments because he could not think of any of his relatives as "class enemies." His mother apparently had little respect for those who held power and opposed his party career. The ambivalence this created contributed to his later skepticism about ideology and enabled him to adapt his views to changing circumstances, adopt reform policies, and eventually reject communist ideology.[1]

The excesses of the Stalinist era further contributed to Shevardnadze's skepticism about ideology. His father had been arrested and briefly imprisoned in 1937, and the father of his own wife, Nanuli, was executed as an "enemy of the people." Nanuli initially rejected Shevardnadze's marriage proposal, fearing her background would ruin his career. Indeed, Shevardnadze had reason to believe she was right. Yegor Ligachev, who later would become Shevardnadze's strongest opponent in the Politburo, had a similar background. His father-in-law had been executed during the Stalin years, and Ligachev wrote: "Such facts had to remain in your personal dossier. I knew of people who had been severely punished for concealing such details of their biography. . . . A person marked with such an entry in his personal file was considered second-class. One could be reminded of this invisible stigma . . . hanging over the family."[2]

Shevardnadze, the youngest of five children, showed early promise as a student, and his parents urged him to become a physician. After completing preliminary medical training, however, he opted for politics, graduating from the party school in Tbilisi in 1951 and the Kutaisi Pedagogical Institute in 1960 with a degree in history. His mother never forgave him for his decision to become a politician, according to Shevardnadze. Shortly before her death, she reproached him, saying he should have tried to ease physical suffering, such as that of his oldest brother Evgrafii, a journalist crippled by polio, rather than taking on the impossible task of curing the ills of society. Shevardnadze asserts that this reproach spurred him to try to prove that his goals were not impossible and that social ills could be treated.[3]

EARLY CAREER

Rapid Rise

While Shevardnadze's early career paralleled that of other Soviet party leaders, in many ways it was unusual and dramatic. Georgia, a republic of five million people, was unique among Soviet republics. Home of Joseph Stalin, Georgia was radically transformed by the dictator's harsh policies of collectivization and repression. Stalin's "war on the peasantry," the collectivization of Georgia's peasant farms in the 1930s, was the most radical transformation of land tenure and village life in Georgia's history. Village institutions of government were eliminated and replaced by Soviets; decision-making was put in the hands of party members responsible to their comrades in Tbilisi and Moscow, not to their local constituents. Georgia became industrialized and urbanized as a result of this assault on the peasantry.[4]

At the same time, Georgia was the fiefdom of Stalin's secret police chief, Lavrenti Beria. Having begun his career in the Georgian secret police, Beria served as head of the party in Georgia from 1931 to 1938. He became head of the Soviet State Committee for Internal Affairs (NKVD) in 1938 but maintained control over the Caucasus until his death in 1953. He directed the great purge of 1936–38 from Georgia, where the toll was extraordinarily high. Nonetheless, in subsequent years his involvement allowed Georgia somewhat more autonomy than other republics.[5]

In the 1950s, the Georgians had considerable control over their own political and economic affairs and an environment of ethnic favoritism existed, which fostered the development of illegal economic networks. Many Georgians accumulated great wealth, while ethnic minorities fared less well and the republic itself grew at a very slow rate. Corruption and black-marketeering existed throughout the Soviet Union, but, according to one observer, "Georgia has a reputation second to none. . . . In form this activity may not differ greatly from what takes place in other regions, but in Georgia it seems to have been carried out on an unparalleled scale and with unrivaled scope and daring."[6] With its freewheeling politics and chronic corruption, Georgia provided a wide-open but dangerous proving ground for a young, ambitious politician.

Shevardnadze's spectacular rise from obscurity to the highest position in Georgia in 1972 is a story of raw ambition, unusual initiative, and brilliant infighting. His career began normally enough: he joined the Communist Party of the Soviet Union (CPSU) in 1948, when he was twenty, and rose steadily through the ranks of the Georgian Communist Youth League (Komsomol), serving as second secretary and first secretary from 1956 until 1961. In 1961, he was released as Komsomol Chief and removed from the Georgian Communist Party's politbureau because he had offended a senior official.[7] Given his proclivity for activism, such a setback probably was inevitable at some point in his career, and he endured several years of obscurity with a regional party organization before returning to Tbilisi as first secretary of a city district in 1963.

Shevardnadze moved out of the party apparatus and into the Georgian security organization as first deputy minister of internal affairs in 1964, becoming minister the following year.[8] His successful anticorruption campaign, supported by Moscow, led to his appointment as second secretary of the Georgian Communist Party in 1972. Once again, he served only briefly in the number-two position, replacing Vasily Mzhavanadze, a long-time crony of Nikita Khrushchev and an alternate member of the CPSU's Politburo, as first secretary the same year. He was only forty-four years old at the time, and he would hold the position of Georgian party leader until his appointment as foreign minister in July 1985.[9]

Exploiting the Battle Against Corruption

Shevardnadze's rapid rise in Georgia was the result of his dramatic campaign against corruption in the republic—an overwhelming and, many would argue, impossible undertaking. Mzhavanadze, a weak and corrupt leader and the most prominent victim of this crusade, had run Georgia since the late 1950s, tolerating if not encouraging black-marketeering, extortion, nepotism, and bribery. Even the agricultural system encouraged corruption. Inadequate remuneration for state farming and shortages of agricultural products in Russia led Georgians to cultivate private plots and create black-market enterprises. A well-oiled system of payoffs and bribery permitted Georgian peasants to send their produce north into the cities of the Russian republic with virtually no accountability to state authorities.

When Shevardnadze returned to a party position in Tbilisi in 1963, he successfully challenged the local rackets and took on one of the most powerful and corrupt officials, Otari Lolashvili, the first secretary of the Tbilisi party committee.[10] His success in sending Lolashvili to prison led to his appointment to the Ministry of the Interior, where he continued his battle against corruption. Shevardnadze's use of unorthodox tactics became legendary in Georgia.[11] According to one account, he packed a suitcase full of the evidence he had collected during his years as interior minister and took it to Moscow. The evidence proved that the corruption permeating Georgia reached as high as Mzhavanadze and his wife, Victoria, who was notorious for her involvement in numerous illicit activities, including the theft of religious treasures from the Georgian patriarchate in Tbilisi.[12] The operation finished Mzhavanadze and demonstrated to leaders in the Kremlin that Shevardnadze was a young man of considerable skill and promise.

Shevardnadze's campaign against Mzhavanadze demonstrated both his willingness to go after those who stood in his way and his effectiveness in doing so. His actions were politically astute and carefully organized—and not without risk. He consistently took the rhetorical high ground on ethical issues, seeking to tarnish his rivals with often-accurate charges of malfeasance. He gained maximum personal and political gain from such campaigns, especially against Mzhavanadze, whose fall opened the position of first secretary for his taking.

Shevardnadze's personal style was well suited to his crusade against corruption. He lived modestly in an unpretentious home and, unlike most republic leaders, did not display his power and position. He was careful to avoid potential conflicts of interest. When he became party first secretary in 1972, he insisted that his brother, Ippokrat, a party official in Georgia, resign as the party's chief of trade, planning, and finance to avoid charges of nepotism.[13] Eduard Shevardnadze had a seemingly natural tendency toward self-righteousness and had little trouble making difficult decisions and implementing them. He made it clear he would purge offenders and show "no mercy to bribe-takers and extortionists," and that is what he did.[14] Perhaps most important, he was willing to take risks and to pursue his goals ruthlessly.

As interior minister, Shevardnadze arrested more than 25,000 people, including 17,000 members of the Communist Party, numerous government ministers, and 70 KGB officials.[15] He was responsible for the torture and execution of many innocent people, including dissidents. This campaign and the purges he initiated as first secretary earned him the undying enmity of many Georgians. They also won him greater notice in Moscow.

MOSCOW CONNECTIONS

All Soviet careers depended on patronage, and Shevardnadze could not have prevailed without help from Moscow. Alexander Shelepin, Soviet

Komsomol Chief and then Chief of the State Committee for Security (KGB) and a member of the Politburo, was Shevardnadze's first important patron, fostering the young man's rise in Georgia's Komsomol. Soviet Minister of the Interior Nikolay Shchelokov embraced Shevardnadze and advocated his appointment as Georgian First Secretary. The Georgian impressed General Secretaries Leonid Brezhnev, Yury Andropov, Konstantin Chernenko, and of course Mikhail Gorbachev with his fight against corruption. Shevardnadze cultivated all these men, using their patronage to gain the greatest possible advantage for himself.

Shchelokov, a close friend of Brezhnev, was a particularly important patron. He became head of the Soviet Ministry of Internal Affairs (MVD) in 1966 and established close contacts with the regional ministry of interior leaders, including Shevardnadze.[16] Ties to Shchelokov, and through him to Brezhnev and Chernenko, led Shevardnadze to support the latter during the struggle for leadership that began before Brezhnev's death in November 1982. The first phase of that struggle, however, was won by Andropov, former chairman of the KGB, who succeeded Brezhnev and laid the foundations for perestroika. Shevardnadze immediately switched his support to Andropov.

Playing the Game

Shevardnadze's effusive praise of party leaders, particularly the general secretary, was widely noticed during his rise through the hierarchy. All Soviet officials paid homage to their seniors, but Shevardnadze was particularly obsequious. He was the first to lavish praise on Brezhnev at the 25th Party Congress in 1976—the zenith of Brezhnev's cult of personality—referring to Brezhnev as *vozhd* (leader), a term previously reserved for Stalin.[17] Shevardnadze was exceeded in his truckling only by Andrey Kirilenko (Brezhnev's heir apparent at the time) and Azerbaijan's Gaydar Aliyev.[18] Ligachev, Shevardnadze's rival, has ridiculed the Georgian's performance:

> I don't recall a single case when Shevardnadze contradicted a *gensek* (general secretary). During the years when Brezhnev was seriously ill and barely functioning, there was a kind of ritual glorification of him by the other leaders. . . . From the vantage point of hindsight, we justly condemn this, but . . . politics is

politics and . . . anyone who wanted to do his job . . . had to pay
tribute in this ritual. . . . But there were true virtuosi who based
their careers on this ritual, and, among them, Shevardnadze was
the best.[19]

By 1979, Shevardnadze had begun his accolades to Chernenko, presumably because of the latter's close ties to Brezhnev and his position as
heir apparent. Even then, Andropov should have been a more attractive
candidate for Shevardnadze. The two men shared a strong anticorruption
agenda, and Andropov's commitment to revitalizing the Soviet economy
complemented Shevardnadze's agenda. But ambition, and Shevardnadze's
perception of where his best chances lay, prevailed, and at a party
meeting in May 1982 Shevardnadze praised Chernenko's "great theoretical and practical work" in "developing party democracy and strengthening party organizations."[20] In October, Chernenko flew to Tbilisi to
present the city with the Order of Lenin and return Shevardnadze's
flattery.

Shevardnadze did not switch to Andropov until the latter became
general secretary. Fearing that he might suffer from his earlier support for
Chernenko, Shevardnadze became the first republic leader to praise the
new leader. In a speech in Tbilisi, he referred to the Politburo as "headed
by Yury Vladimirovich Andropov"—a controversial description that
had been adopted for Brezhnev only after he clearly had risen above
his colleagues.[21]

Andropov quickly signaled his appreciation of Shevardnadze's policies
in Georgia. His choice for first secretary of the Russian Republic was
Gennady Kolbin, who had been Shevardnadze's second secretary in
Tbilisi and was an expert in the fight against corruption. Andropov's
battle with corruption in the Soviet Union was based, at least in
part, on Shevardnadze's struggles in Georgia. According to Andropov's
biographers, he was "enchanted by the effectiveness and inventiveness
displayed in the Georgian version of a police state."[22] Andropov also
personally intervened to save several Georgian experiments in economic
reform from being choked by the bureaucracy in Moscow.[23]

When Andropov died in February 1984, Chernenko succeeded him.
True to form, Shevardnadze quickly referred to Chernenko as "head of
the Politburo" and praised him lavishly.[24] While all party leaders spoke
in support of party unity and cohesion following Chernenko's election,
Shevardnadze's endorsement, once again, was particularly effusive. It is

hardly surprising, given his history, that in the succession struggle that followed Chernenko's death in March 1985, Shevardnadze emerged as one of the most enthusiastic supporters of the victor, Mikhail Gorbachev.

Shevardnadze's behavior during the succession crises that occurred from 1982 to 1985 revealed a high degree of ambition, a well-developed sense of how the political game was played, and an ability to change his tune rapidly when he had mistakenly endorsed the losing candidate. This performance provided no indication of moral leadership or courage. On the contrary, it demonstrated political agility, opportunism, and seemingly unrestrained ambition.

Shevardnadze's Rationale

Shevardnadze justified his loyalty to the Soviet system and its leaders on two grounds: first, belief in the system, and later the need to protect his reformist agenda. His support for the system originally was based on his perception that Stalin and the party had led the Soviet Union to victory in the Great Patriotic War (World War II) in which his older brother, Akaki, had died: "The war with fascism became a personal battle to me. The fascists were attacking Communism, and Communism was my religion. The victory in that war became the victory of Communism, and that meant my own personal victory."[25] Shevardnadze even believed that the terror he witnessed in Georgia during the Stalin years had occurred without Stalin's knowledge and that the leadership in Moscow remained committed to improving the life of the people. In 1991, he stated that he eventually came to believe otherwise: "We all carry the burden of our past. We have experienced Stalin, Khrushchev, Brezhnev, Andropov, and Chernenko. We made speeches, praised them. I even composed a poem praising Stalin when I was young. But we change, life requires us to do so."[26]

Having denounced Stalin and his excesses when it was politically desirable to do so, Shevardnadze was able to change course again when he felt political necessity beckon. On May 7, 1995, on the eve of his departure for Moscow to celebrate the 50th anniversary of V-E Day, he visited Stalin's birthplace in Gori to emphasize his Georgian "roots" and pay homage to a fellow Georgian.

Nevertheless, Shevardnadze has claimed that he became disillusioned with the Soviet system in the 1950s. Like many Soviets, he was shaken by Khrushchev's speech in 1956 describing Stalin's crimes, particularly the campaign of terror. He was horrified when Georgian demonstrators, protesting what they considered the affront to Georgian pride in Khrushchev's speech, were mowed down by machine-gun fire. "I used to write letters to Khrushchev," Shevardnadze said, but "then he sent tanks to Tbilisi and 150 students died."[27] Describing his reaction to these events, Shevardnadze wrote: "It is agonizingly difficult to acknowledge that you have worshipped the wrong god, that you have been deceived. It shattered my life and my faith."[28] According to Shevardnadze, "comrades sent from Moscow" had accused the demonstrators of "bourgeois nationalism." He spoke out against these accusations, he said, arguing that dismissing the protesters as nationalists was morally reprehensible and politically dangerous.[29]

Shevardnadze believed that members of his generation had acquired a "1956 complex" for the rest of their lives—rejecting the use of force as a political instrument.[30] Commitment to the nonuse of force became one of his most important contributions to the end of communism and the Cold War, permitting the virtually nonviolent demise of the Soviet empire and the bloodless dissolution of the Soviet Union itself. Shevardnadze opposed the use of force in Tbilisi in 1989 and in the Baltics in 1990. In his resignation speech in December 1990, he predicted that the use of force would undermine perestroika. The violence in Lithuania three weeks later proved him right.

Shevardnadze's second justification for "playing the game" was that it was necessary if he were to have a chance to reform the system.[31] In an emotional speech after being harshly criticized at the Party Congress in July 1990, Shevardnadze described the environment in which he had operated as

> a system where a certain selection of words represents a ritual sign of devotion to that system—and if you fail to do homage to it you run the risk of being deprived of any opportunity to do anything. . . . God forbid you ever say anything contrary to the ritual. You'll be an anathema in an instant. To have an opportunity of doing anything my way, I was quite frequently forced to speak like everyone else. For instance, that meant paying homage to the "number one.". . . I say this with sadness, recognizing the definite moral damage implicit in such an admission. But I am saying it, . . . and let he who has not experienced this split

personality cast the first stone. . . . These "rules of the game" made no provision for any exception. There was just one way out—not taking part.[32]

Shevardnadze would later claim that he took many risks to pursue his policies: "A great deal of what we did in the republic party organization was contrary to top-level directives and rejected all-powerful centralism as a principle. There was a great risk inherent in this willfulness and it was often intimated to me that I might have to pay for it."[33]

Much of Shevardnadze's subsequent justification for his behavior was self-serving, but it also truthfully reflected the way things were done. Certainly he was an opportunist, particularly good at the political game. At the same time, during his thirteen years as Georgia's leader he took innovative steps to improve the economy and reform the system, learning lessons that he eventually applied to the Soviet Union. He truckled to Moscow and he repressed dissidents and nationalists, but he also reformed some of the worst aspects of the system.

REFORMER AND INNOVATOR

Shevardnadze's willingness to challenge his party bosses when it came to policy and reform contradicts his opportunistic image. When he became republic leader, his primary objectives were to galvanize a staggering economy and attack rampant corruption. His record as a republic leader was impressive in many respects, and it presaged characteristics he would demonstrate and policies he would pursue as foreign minister.

Economic Reform

Shevardnadze's Georgia was one of the only republics in the Soviet Union that undertook real economic reform and achieved economic growth. In the first two years of his tenure as party chief, industrial output in Georgia rose 9.6 percent and agricultural output rose more than 18 percent.[34] Food queues disappeared in Tbilisi but lengthened in Moscow.[35] Some of his programs were adopted by the Soviet government and introduced throughout the country.

Unlike most Soviet officials, Shevardnadze was unafraid to sound like a capitalist, arguing that "it is simply laughable to be afraid of economic incentives."[36] His flexible agricultural policies were designed to reward individual initiative, an approach not consistent with classic Marxist-Leninist doctrine—and they worked. He endorsed privatization, giving rein to entrepreneurial spirit by allowing consumer enterprises to run on semiprivate lines and making Georgia the first republic to allow family ownership of small private enterprises.[37]

The showcase of Shevardnadze's agricultural reform was the Abasha experiment, created in a backward region in western Georgia in 1973. Shevardnadze regrouped all agricultural institutions into one management association and introduced a new system of remuneration based on a Hungarian model. Hungary had taken the lead in Eastern Europe during the 1970s, implementing agricultural reforms that included giving incentives to those who performed well and returning decision-making to local levels. In Abasha, Shevardnadze gave collective farm workers a percentage of the payment for plan fulfillment in the form of a share of the crop. The experiment, which resulted in spectacular increases in agricultural production, was extended to other regions of the republic and became the model for so-called RAPOs (agricultural-industrial associations), created at the national level in 1982.

In 1981, Shevardnadze announced that "the first steps towards applying the experience of the Hungarian Peoples Republic have yielded very good results."[38] He visited Hungary, where he announced that the Hungarians had found "an ideal solution in the relationship between agricultural cooperatives and household farms that is advantageous to everyone."[39]

Shevardnadze also created a new management approach, combining ministries and state committees into one State Committee for Agricultural Production in order to give more authority to local officials and escape the bureaucratic tentacles of the ministries.[40] Other experiments involved coordination of planning and consolidation of ministries in order to strengthen local authorities. Economic experiments that had withered elsewhere in the face of bureaucratic inertia at the center flourished under Shevardnadze.

Shevardnadze took credit for improving the economic performance in Georgia: "Without false modesty it is possible to state that . . . our republic has been turned into a proving ground for economic experiments, the resonance and significance of which, thanks to the support and approval of all-union organs, extends far beyond the borders of

Georgia."[41] He emphasized his commitment to innovation and experimentation:

> We . . . decided not to limit people—let them seek and they shall find. If something does not turn out right, the republic will not perish. Failure is also experience. In economic matters, of course, you cannot do without sober calculation, but you also cannot do without courage and even risk at times. These qualities are necessary not only in extraordinary circumstances, but also in everyday life.[42]

Only seven months before his appointment as foreign minister, Shevardnadze claimed that there were more than thirty economic experiments operating in Georgia. While not all would be successful, all would provide experience and contribute to economic reform. He believed that the key to progress was expanding and deepening the democratic basis of management as well as encouraging initiative and competition.[43] This pragmatic, activist approach in Georgia foreshadowed his later pragmatism as foreign minister.

Continued Attacks on Corruption

Throughout his tenure as Georgia's leader, Shevardnadze challenged corruption and graft. Black-marketeering and bribery continued to be fundamental elements of the Soviet Union's second economy, and Georgia remained second to none. Only 68 percent of agricultural goods produced in Georgia in the early 1970s were marketed legally, compared with nearly 100 percent in the rest of the Caucasus. Business in Georgia meant "favoritism, parochialism, cronyism, and careerism . . . on the basis of family ties and corruption." Family members exploited the positions of high-ranking relatives, and state problems were considered in a "narrow circle of relatives, family, or close friends."[44]

Various anecdotes illustrate Shevardnadze's unusual approach to attacking problems. He went on television to deliver angry attacks on black-marketeers and set up an Institute for the Study of Public Opinion to rally public support for a cleanup campaign.[45] He even indulged in subterfuge to ferret out wrongdoing. Shortly after issuing an order that no produce be exported from the republic, he dressed as a peasant and drove a car filled with tomatoes toward the border. He successfully bribed policemen at each checkpoint—then conducted a purge of the police. In another incident, Shevardnadze is said to have asked his colleagues to vote on an issue with their left hands; he then commented on their fancy foreign watches and suggested that they go out and replace them with Soviet watches.[46] Shevardnadze has neither confirmed nor denied these stories; whether true or not, they served his interest, portraying him as an imaginative battler of systemic corruption—long before it became part of the national agenda.

Shevardnadze maintained his anticorruption agenda after becoming Soviet foreign minister. He realized that many returning diplomats brought home expensive equipment such as tape recorders, cameras, and videos—and failed to report their purchases. At a collegium meeting of the foreign ministry, he announced that this practice was unacceptable and that there would be an accounting; offenders would be demoted or dismissed.[47] He also launched an attack on nepotism in the foreign ministry and the institutes associated with it, resulting in the dismissal of numerous leading officials.

Political Experimentation

Shevardnadze encouraged and protected political experimentation in Georgia. He created high-level bodies to oversee new projects and introduced a system for the study, analysis, and molding of public opinion, coordinated by an institute attached to the Georgian Central Committee. The institute worked closely with the media to provide television interviews with government ministers during which the public could submit questions.[48] In his own policy of glasnost, he held regular meetings with the press and urged open discussion of political and economic problems.

Although effusive in his praise of Moscow's leaders, Shevardnadze criticized such flattery in Georgia. He urged delegates to party congresses to be honest and to offer criticism of all officials, including himself, so that mistakes might be corrected. In July 1983, at the plenum of the Central Committee of the Georgian party, Shevardnadze declared: "When I call upon comrades to point out shortcomings in the functioning of the central committee, then of course I have in mind the work of the first secretary as well. Like any other human being I have my faults, and

I would like members of the central committee to point them out."[49] This attitude was unusual in a Soviet leader, and it reflected Shevardnadze's recognition that the terrible excesses resulting from Stalin's personality cult had occurred because the leader (*vozhd*) was portrayed as infallible and no challenge to his authority or policies was tolerated. While the terror of the Stalin years had ended, the stultifying effects of the cult of personality persisted throughout the Soviet system.[50]

In calling for a new relationship between party leaders and subordinates, arguing that it was necessary that power come from below, Shevardnadze also was ahead of his time. He acknowledged: "From this come well-known difficulties. One . . . leader prophesied about himself: 'This democratization of yours will end up with my being removed from work.' And that is what happened. There is nothing that can be done about it; democratic power is the power of the people, and the people are just and strict."[51]

One of Shevardnadze's most courageous acts as first secretary was his sponsorship of the movie *Repentance* by the late Georgian director Tengiz Abuladze, who created a metaphor for the horrors of the Stalin era in his film. Shevardnadze wrote: "The very title of the film . . . presupposes . . . recognition of personal responsibility."[52] The protagonist in the film is a tyrant, with high leather boots like Stalin's, a black shirt like Mussolini's, a mustache like Hitler's, and a pince-nez reminiscent of Beria. When the movie was finally shown in 1986, it was described as "the most important event in Soviet cultural life in at least a decade."[53]

When he approved production of the film, Shevardnadze had not been confident it would be released, but he accepted the risk because he believed it should be produced. The film was completed in the early 1980s but impounded by authorities in Moscow. Shevardnadze felt guilty, knowing he had abandoned Abuladze by not fighting the decision to impound the film. He later brought the situation to Gorbachev's attention in 1985. After reviewing the film, Gorbachev agreed that it should be released. The full Politburo finally approved the release, although many predicted—correctly, as it turned out—that it would precipitate a chain reaction of historical revision.[54]

Shevardnadze arranged for the world premiere of *Repentance* in Tbilisi in November 1986 and later sponsored a screening for Western correspondents at Moscow's House of Film. According to his press spokesman Gennady Gerasimov, Shevardnadze was disappointed that the Western press corps did not appear to understand the political and historical significance of the film.[55] His approach to *Repentance* foreshadowed his subsequent support for the publication of Boris Pasternak's *Doctor Zhivago* and the release of the Soviet Union's most famous dissident, Andrey Sakharov, several of the more dramatic steps taken by the new leadership to demonstrate its commitment to the new policy of openness (*glasnost*).[56]

Shevardnadze's efforts to introduce reform in Georgia were not universally popular, and he was occasionally in personal danger. His physical courage, seen on numerous occasions, has never been questioned. In 1977, a Georgian crowd disagreed when the Russian referee's call gave the advantage to a visiting soccer team from Voroshilograd; the crowd poured onto the field, threatening the referee. Shevardnadze waded into the mob to end the confrontation. During Shevardnadze's tenure as interior minister, an armed criminal barricaded himself in a house that was quickly surrounded by police. Dressed as a general, Shevardnadze walked to the house and demanded that the man come out and surrender his weapon—and the man did so. Shevardnadze later said that he had not been afraid; he assumed the man would take the presence of a general as a compliment and would not shoot. In 1978, during serious clashes between Georgians and Abkhazians, Shevardnadze again confronted an angry mob, demanding an end to the violence.[57] He demonstrated similar courage during the war of secession in Abkhazia in 1993, when he stayed in the besieged city of Sukhumi despite the clear personal danger.

Balanced Approach to Georgian Nationalism

Georgia is unique. Mediterranean and cosmopolitan, Georgians traditionally lived by looser rules than other Soviets. In his battles against corruption and for reform, Shevardnadze was taking on generations of easy virtue, underground capitalism, and heavy drinking. He also was taking on a strongly nationalistic republic, with a contradictory history of tolerance and ethnic favoritism. Georgians, individualistic and freedom-loving, did not give in easily.

Shevardnadze's attitude toward Georgian nationalism is highly controversial. He owed his position to the leadership in Moscow, and he became the agent for carrying out Brezhnev's policy of Russification. Many Georgians have never forgiven him for telling the 25th Congress of the Georgian Communist Party that "for Georgians, the sun rises not in the east, but in the north—in Russia."[58] He had to walk a narrow line between Soviet authorities and his reform agenda in Georgia, which required him to mollify officials in both Moscow and Tbilisi as well as the public at large.

Along with corruption and inefficiency, Shevardnadze targeted what he termed "extreme nationalism" as one of the major obstacles to economic prosperity and social well-being in Georgia. He condemned both "national narrow-mindedness and isolation" and writers and artists who exploited themes with nationalist overtones. During the 1970s, dissident nationalism became a phenomenon in Georgia as intellectuals reacted to the corruption of the system. Among these dissidents was Zviad Gamsakhurdia, son of the prominent writer Konstantin Gamsakhurdia. Gamsakhurdia would become a longtime rival of Shevardnadze and the first elected president of independent Georgia in 1991.

During Shevardnadze's years as first secretary, nationalist sentiment was high. Emotions focused particularly on protection of the Georgian language, seen as being under attack from Moscow. The spring of 1978 saw a dramatic mass demonstration in Tbilisi against an ill-advised attempt, based on policy dictated by Moscow, to withdraw the traditional clause in the Georgian constitution affirming Georgian as the sole state language. Hundreds of students demonstrated in front of Central Committee headquarters. Shevardnadze condescendingly called down to them, "My children, what are you doing?" They responded, "We're not your children. Go to Moscow, where both your children and your parents are."[59]

Shevardnadze, who had requested instructions from the Kremlin about how to handle the demonstration, finally decided to act on his own. He asked some of his colleagues to come with him to talk to the demonstrators, but they were afraid to face the angry crowd. Shevardnadze went alone to address the demonstrators. His arguments failed to win them over, and he ultimately supported their protest; with Moscow's acquiescence, he told the demonstrators that Georgian would remain the only official language of the republic. The incident ended, and Georgia adopted a constitution that conformed with the demands of the students.[60] At the same time, however, legislation was passed in Moscow that called for increasing the level of Russian language training in non-Russian republics. The resulting tension led to further demonstrations.

Minority groups within Georgia also were active. Many had long-standing claims to autonomy themselves, and all resented the favoritism shown to Georgians in the republic. The Abkhaz, for example, who made up only 16 percent of their own autonomous republic, created problems that worsened in the post-Soviet period. They resented Georgian dominance and demanded that Abkhazia be transferred to the republic of Russia. In December 1977, a group of Abkhaz intellectuals wrote to Brezhnev, demanding that the republic be allowed to secede from Georgia. Ivan Kapitonov, a Central Committee Secretary, was sent from Moscow to calm the situation. Various concessions were made to the secessionists, including the building of an Abkhaz university and television station and the expansion of Abkhaz publications.

Unlike most Georgian politicians, Shevardnadze understood the need for these concessions and made it clear that he would not tolerate the exploitation of other ethnic groups in the republic by allowing unfettered Georgian nationalism. He was careful to protect the rights of minorities, even accommodating the interests of the small Greek minority in the republic.[61] This basic tolerance would be reflected in his career as foreign minister when he implemented a human rights agenda, both in order to improve relations with the United States and because he believed it was the correct policy.

On this issue, as in his effusive praise for party leaders, Shevardnadze demonstrated his ability to balance the interests and pressures of differing constituencies and to act as mediator. Whether because of his policies or in spite of them, there was a cultural renaissance in Georgia during his tenure. A new mood of optimism was reflected in the nationalist sentiment of many literary works of the period. The improving economy contributed to this sense of optimism, as did the cultural concessions granted to Georgia by Moscow during Shevardnadze's tenure.[62]

Shevardnadze's balanced approach to Georgian nationalism antagonized those who were more extreme in attitude. In the eyes of many, Shevardnadze represented the rule of Moscow. This perception was reinforced by the fact that he came from the Guria region of Georgia. Many political struggles in Georgia can be traced to rivalry between Georgians from the Guria region and their close neighbors in Mingrelia.[63] Most of the social-democrats who founded the independent state of Georgia that lasted from 1918 to 1921 were Mingrels; most of the Bolsheviks, who removed them, were Guris. Thus, in the eyes of many Georgian nationalists Shevardnadze had his heritage as well as his policies to overcome.

THE NEGATIVE LEGACY OF REPRESSION

The most serious charge against Shevardnadze during his years as republic leader was that he arrested, tortured, and executed political dissidents in Georgia. While he earned praise for his crackdown against corruption, many Georgians hated him for his purges of politicians and dissidents. As he attacked those who did not agree with his positions and policies, Shevardnadze's rhetoric was harsh. In 1974, he said that little progress was being made against "outworn traditions—religion, nationalism, the psychology of property," and he called on everyone to watch everyone else.[64] He created overlapping systems of control involving state and party watchdog agencies.

The reaction to Shevardnadze's crackdown on opponents was a wave of violence. Beginning in 1972, there were demonstrations, bombings, and attempts against his life. One such attempt almost succeeded; at the final moment the would-be assassin, Shevardnadze's chauffeur, aimed the gun at his own head and fired. A fire destroyed the beautiful Paliashvili Theater of Opera and Ballet only hours before Shevardnadze was scheduled to appear to celebrate the anniversary of the end of World War II.

The history of political dissent in Georgia is an old one, and dissent remained strong during the Shevardnadze years, as did its repression. Dissidents maintained contact with human rights activists in Moscow and created their own human rights groups in Georgia. Two *samizdat* journals, the *Golden Fleece* and the *Georgian Herald,* appeared in the mid-1970s. Georgian human rights activists organized a Helsinki monitoring group in 1977 to observe compliance with the provisions of the 1975 Helsinki Final Act. Most of the Georgian monitors were arrested within a few months and sentenced to imprisonment and internal exile.[65]

As late as May 1982, Shevardnadze participated in a meeting of Georgian party leaders and officials to call for increased vigilance in fighting the subversive influence of Western ideology and in halting criticism of his policies. Several months earlier he had charged that the republic had not established a healthy moral-political atmosphere and called for an intensification of the campaign against "all demagogues, . . . unhealthy elements, people to whom nothing is sacred, who do not perceive anything good in our life."[66] He presumably was concerned with religious and nationalist sentiment, particularly among students. Students had played a prominent role in the demonstrations that took place in Georgia in 1978 and 1981. Attacks on those having a "pernicious influence" on youth were aimed at Shevardnadze's antagonist, Zviad Gamsakhurdia, who was named as one of the participants in the demonstration in October 1981. Shevardnadze's condemnation of the activities of "would-be champions of the people, slanderers, and demagogues" on at least three occasions between December and mid-January 1983 also was aimed at Gamsakhurdia.[67]

Gamsakhurdia, who collected *samizdat* documents that reached the West during the 1970s, charged that Shevardnadze personally had authorized the torture of political prisoners when he was minister of internal affairs. Those charges were confirmed by victims as well as by several of those carrying out the torture.[68]

While Shevardnadze's actions brought some improvement to law and order in Georgia, things remained far from perfect. In 1982, republic leaders were still focusing on economic crimes and parasitism, stating that there had been no decisive breakthroughs. Shevardnadze's campaign to eradicate corruption in Georgia was an ongoing, unfinished struggle, and when he returned to Georgia in 1992 he found a society still functioning in the old freewheeling, corrupt manner.

A former Georgian dissident has provided some insight into Shevardnadze's personality and performance as party leader. Alexandr Potskhishvili, who suffered persecution under Shevardnadze, said that he had believed in Shevardnadze's principles and had fought "in defense of the truth," thinking that he would be protected. Instead, he was arrested, sentenced to a year of forced labor, and kicked out of his institute. For seven years, he tried to talk to the first secretary but was consistently told that "Shevardnadze does not want to see you." In spite of Shevardnadze's past actions against the Georgian people and himself, Potskhishvili would argue that Georgia needed Shevardnadze in 1992. Only Shevardnadze was capable of leading Georgia out of the abyss, and, "however bitter I may be, I cannot but welcome his return."[69]

Jaba Ioseliani, a dissident (and also a former bank robber and future leader of the paramilitary force Mkhedrioni in newly independent Georgia) was jailed in the 1970s when Shevardnadze was Georgian minister of internal affairs. However, Ioseliani later defended Shevardnadze, saying that it is not always necessary to fight the system from the outside, that you could fight it from within and above—as Shevardnadze did.[70] Ioseliani indicated that Shevardnadze, as interior minister, had intervened on his behalf. Ioseliani had been released from jail in 1966 and was invited to visit the United States. He heard that Shevardnadze sympathized with his application and went to see him. Shevardnadze promised that he would try to help, but that he probably would not get approval for the trip. Ioseliani was denied the trip, but the military officer who returned his papers told him that Shevardnadze had come three times personally to intervene on his behalf, something that had never happened before.

RETROSPECTIVE

Shevardnadze has admitted that he did not accomplish as much as he should have during his years in Georgia. The totalitarian state is a penitentiary with horrifying features, he argued, and it is beyond the power of one man to reform it without changing the nature of the state. "What's done is done. . . . I was forced to make unpopular decisions." He has insisted, however, that he was thinking and working in the right direction by challenging the excessive dictatorship of the central agencies and the dominance of the command-administrative system—and that what he did could have been characterized as anti-Soviet by the prevailing standards of that time.[71] Admitting that the dissidents were normal people angry with the existing order, Shevardnadze has claimed that he corrected some things and kept some people out of harm's way.

Clearly sensitive to criticism of his repression of dissent, Shevardnadze has stated that such repression was part of Moscow's policy and that he could have done little to change the policy. But he also admits he should have done more: "Could I have prevented this or stopped it? Of course not. But I was obligated to protest. At the time, however, in the 1970s, I was not prepared to do so, either inwardly—psychologically—or politically."[72]

Shevardnadze has claimed that he did not find it easy to stand up to authority. For years he accepted the legitimacy of the system and its leaders and only gradually developed his own system of values and the ability to take a stand. When Gorbachev announced his antialcohol campaign in 1985, Shevardnadze claimed he was horrified because of the impact this campaign might have on the Georgian economy. He himself had maintained a vineyard during his years in Georgia and understood its importance to Georgia's economy and its way of life. And yet he voted in favor of the policy, which suggested a weakness of character:

> To this day, I can muster the determination to act in an uncompromising manner only after a long struggle with myself. I will not hasten to speak out until the right "critical mass" of willpower and thought spills over into a decision. This is a serious drawback for a politician and for the cause, but I cannot hide it. There is no other way to explain how and why I took so long to reach my present state.[73]

Some observers attribute Shevardnadze's contradictory behavior to more dubious character traits. Former Soviet Ambassador Victor Israelyan describes Shevardnadze as a "great actor" as "every great politician must be." According to Israelyan, Shevardnadze might seem approachable and eager to get to know you, but he "can project any impression he thinks you want." At the same time, he "keeps his distance. He has a big smile, but the smile is artificial." Israelyan has argued that Shevardnadze is a man driven by ambition above all else.[74]

Nevertheless, Shevardnadze had an unusual ability to lead, to take initiative, and to pursue a course of action with courage and determination. Many observers, particularly U.S. Secretaries of State George P. Shultz and James A. Baker III, describe him as a man of exceptional personal charm. One writer describes him as a man of personal modesty, integrity, and a satirical, even impish, sense of humor.[75] He had the instincts and capabilities that every outstanding politician must have to succeed: understanding of the system and knowledge of the moves necessary to get ahead; ability to convince people and draw them into your course of action; pragmatism and adaptability; willingness to work hard; and even charisma.

Shevardnadze took these characteristics with him when he went to Moscow in 1985, bringing fresh air from Georgia to the Soviet foreign ministry. Many experts underestimated his abilities and failed to recognize that his background in Georgia might provide him with a unique view of the world and Moscow's role in it. Most certainly failed to perceive that Shevardnadze would bring to the foreign ministry a commitment to radical change and a willingness to implement reform in an unorthodox manner.

2

EVOLUTION OF A POLITICAL PARTNERSHIP

In Gorbachev, I had a
friend who was always
ready to help me out, in
word and deed.
—Eduard Shevardnadze

Gorbachev's appointment of Shevardnadze as foreign minister was his first shocking decision as general secretary. In turning to a regional party leader with no foreign policy background, Gorbachev was relying on personal instinct and political acumen. His long association with Shevardnadze was rooted in shared frustration with the inefficiencies and corruption of the communist system they served, and he was counting on his colleague to help turn things around. Their five-year partnership, created to revitalize that system, would end by precipitating its destruction.

The relationship between Shevardnadze and Gorbachev was more professional than personal.[1] They shared an obsession to reverse the deterioration of the Soviet Union and to improve its position abroad. Neither man had close personal friends, and both were workaholics. U.S. Ambassador Arthur Hartman remarked that there were times when

Shevardnadze said he "would get back to me later in the evening, then break for dinner and return to the office near midnight to resume work."[2] As first secretary in Georgia, Shevardnadze did not take a vacation in his first nine years on the job.[3] He would take few vacations as foreign minister.

The two men shared many other characteristics. Both were intelligent and tough-minded, tenacious and energetic, hardworking and unpretentious. Both were opposed to corruption; Shevardnadze fought it in Georgia, and Gorbachev was identified with an anticorruption campaign during his career in Stavropol in southern Russia. Both were obviously "quick studies," taking on large conceptual issues in a short period of time. Both were activists and had married extremely intelligent women, although Nanuli Shevardnadze was far more congenial and relaxed than Raisa Gorbachev.

Above all, Gorbachev and Shevardnadze were reformers, very different from their immediate predecessors, Konstantin Chernenko and Andrey Gromyko. The president reformed the entire Soviet system; the foreign minister reformed both the foreign ministry and the Kremlin's approach to diplomacy and foreign policy. Both leaders were responsible for the strategic retreat that led to the end of the Cold War and contributed to the unintended dissolution of the Soviet Union. Both understood the need for change in Eastern Europe, for pursuit of arms control with the West, and for resolution of human rights differences with the United States. Both also recognized the domestic context of foreign policy, particularly the harm done to Moscow's position at home and abroad because of its exaggerated concern with secrecy and security.

The two future leaders had become privately critical of the Soviet system and, in the winter of 1984–85, at Pitsunda on Georgia's Black Sea coast, Gorbachev agreed with Shevardnadze's observation "Everything has gone rotten."[4] By this time, they had been confidants for more than two decades and had discussed every aspect of Soviet policy, both foreign and domestic. When Gorbachev was named to the Politburo, his dacha was located at Pitsunda, which meant the two men had more time to spend together. They often discussed various possibilities for resolving the country's problems, including the need to revitalize the economy, to open the system to criticism and reform, and to gain some breathing room by making adjustments in foreign policy. They agreed that the invasion of Afghanistan had been disastrous and would have to be reversed.

The men used their meetings and conversations to develop new policies, as well as the philosophical and political underpinnings that would make those policies possible. Rebuilding the economy (perestroika) would require more democracy, more openness (glasnost), more humanity. Refocusing foreign policy would involve a fundamental shift in assumptions about the arms race and the structure of the international system, and an end to Soviet isolation from that system. What they were working out was what would eventually become known as "new thinking" in Soviet policy.

"New thinking" derived from the perception that the Soviet system was mired in stagnation and decay. Gorbachev and Shevardnadze were not alone in this perception. The leadership and the intelligentsia had known there were serious problems when Nikita Khrushchev undertook his abortive effort to implement reforms in the 1960s. In 1983, Prime Minister Nikolay Ryzhkov had prepared more than one hundred memorandums on economic reform for General Secretary Yury Andropov. Everyone knew something had to be done; some thought they knew what to do, but few had the inclination or the will to do it.

The genesis of new thinking was pragmatic rather than philosophical; its primary focus was internal rather than external; its goals were limited rather than revolutionary. Neither Gorbachev nor Shevardnadze contemplated rejection of communism or anticipated the radical changes that would occur both at home and abroad as a result of their policies. Rather, they believed the system could be revitalized and preserved. "We agreed that we wanted genuine socialism," Gorbachev noted in 1990.[5]

Gorbachev and Shevardnadze may have had intentions similar to those of President Franklin Delano Roosevelt in the 1930s—that is, to preserve their system through modification and reform. Like Roosevelt, Gorbachev and Shevardnadze were practical politicians, not revolutionaries. Unlike Roosevelt, however, they unleashed forces they could not control and precipitated events that far exceeded their expectations.

As the two men were swept along in the torrent of change their policies precipitated, they adapted and reacted in different ways. Gorbachev equivocated and frequently sought to slow the pace of reform. Shevardnadze, growing skeptical that the old order could be preserved, became increasingly committed to radical change. He eventually parted company with Gorbachev, resigning in December 1990, in large part because his old ally had failed to support his policies and to defend him against harsh criticism. In his resignation speech, Shevardnadze provided a dramatic and, as it turned out, a prescient warning that the Soviet Union was slipping back toward repression, dictatorship, and the use of force.

Finally, Shevardnadze indicated that major differences had developed between Gorbachev and himself about the role of socialism in the Soviet Union. Gorbachev had continued to speak about the "socialist system" and "fidelity to the socialist path of development," but Shevardnadze had gradually ceased making such references. Shevardnadze noted that he had not mentioned socialism for a long time because he had developed "serious doubts" about it.[6] Thus, by the end of the partnership the two men had different visions and different agendas; they had been unable to retain their shared vision.

EARLY FRIENDSHIP

One of Shevardnadze's greatest political strengths was his closeness to Gorbachev. They met in the late 1950s in Moscow, where both were attending a Komsomol Central Committee meeting. They found that they shared many perceptions and views and quickly became confidants. As it was just a short drive through the Caucasus from Gorbachev's home in Stavropol to Shevardnadze's home in Georgia, the two men were able to visit each other often. Throughout the 1960s and 1970s, their careers kept them on parallel paths, giving them opportunities to meet and reinforce their shared perceptions of the backwardness of the Soviet economy.[7]

Gorbachev moved to Moscow to take positions in the party in the late 1970s. Although still based in Tbilisi, Shevardnadze became a candidate (nonvoting) member of the CPSU Politburo in 1978; Gorbachev attained that status the following year. Gorbachev became a full member of the Politburo in 1980, and Shevardnadze became a full member the day before his appointment as foreign minister. Gorbachev's Politburo dacha was located near Pitsunda on the Georgian part of the Black Sea coast, and the two men continued to meet there frequently as well as in Moscow. Shevardnadze found Gorbachev a man of learning and erudition, devoid of the "artificial Komsomol modesty" the Georgian found so annoying. Gorbachev's thinking, according to Shevardnadze, went beyond conventional wisdom.

As their friendship developed, the two men began to speak frankly to each other. Their candor and reliance on each other for discussing politics were reflected in Shevardnadze's account of their meeting after the Soviet invasion of Afghanistan in 1979, which they both privately opposed. When they learned of the invasion, he wrote, they were stunned; each wanting to discuss the situation with a trusted friend, they "hastened to meet."[8]

While in Moscow, Gorbachev supported Shevardnadze's experiments in Georgia. As party secretary in charge of agriculture for the Soviet Union, Gorbachev was particularly interested in Shevardnadze's efforts to increase agricultural production by allowing more local autonomy and encouraging the use of incentives. He watched the successes of the Abasha experiment to reward the initiative of collective farmers and the amalgamation of agricultural ministries. Gorbachev visited Georgia on several occasions in the early 1980s and was impressed by what he saw. After the last visit, in 1984, he publicly endorsed the Abasha experiment.[9]

Shevardnadze and Gorbachev frequently commented to each other that it was necessary to ignore Marxist-Leninist ideology in order to achieve "real progress," suggesting growing skepticism about the validity of the communist model and recognition of the need to modify its precepts.[10] They wanted to democratize the system and abandon many of the failed practices of the past. Doing so meant taking on the system, with its layers of bureaucratic inertia and corruption.

The issue that created the strongest bond between Gorbachev and Shevardnadze was the desperate need for systemic reform. Gorbachev's patron in the Politburo had been Andropov, whose brief tenure as general secretary in 1982–84 set the agenda for perestroika. During a visit to Washington in 1987, Raisa Gorbachev saw a picture of Andropov and commented, "We owe everything to him."[11] Gorbachev and Shevardnadze discussed the numerous studies that Prime Minister Ryzhkov had organized during the Andropov years, incorporating them into their own thinking about domestic reform.

ONE MAN'S CHOICE

The decision to appoint Shevardnadze foreign minister was made by Gorbachev alone. In his memoirs, Shevardnadze indicates that he was shocked by the announcement:

> Try to describe the feelings of a man who was completely en-
> grossed in the affairs of his little homeland. . . . I had a relief map
> of Georgia in my office. . . . I had never kept any other maps
> around. I had traveled some but not extensively. . . . I did not
> know any foreign languages, only my native Georgian and Rus-
> sian, which I spoke with an ineradicable accent. I lacked expe-
> rience.[12]

Shevardnadze also says he told Gorbachev that naming a Georgian to an
international post would be ill-advised: "My nationality was by no means
a side issue. Historically, this post had always been held by either a
Russian or a student of Russian culture with roots in Russia. My appointment would be met with ambivalence in Russia and the other republics.
Some hard questions would inevitably be raised abroad as well."[13] Gorbachev rejected Shevardnadze's suggestion that his inexperience was a
reason for him to remain in Tbilisi, stating that "no experience" might
be a good thing.

Although Shevardnadze had little foreign policy experience in the
conventional sense, his dealings with Moscow as a first secretary of a
struggling republic in the Caucasus required good diplomatic skills and a
firm understanding of negotiating tactics. Moreover, he had traveled to
Europe, the Middle East, Brazil, and India. He had hosted regular visits
of Latin American delegations to Tbilisi. He also had served as a member
of the Soviet Committee for Solidarity with Asian and African Countries
which brought him into contact with foreign delegations.[14]

On the surface it appeared that Shevardnadze would be little more
than a mouthpiece for Gorbachev, who would conduct his own foreign
policy. Shevardnadze's official comments about foreign policy had been
no more than the mandatory attacks on the United States and imperialism and standard support for Soviet positions. He defended Moscow's
involvement in Afghanistan, for example, as its socialist duty. He had
given no clues about his own attitudes or about what policies he
preferred. An American group that had met with Shevardnadze before
his appointment developed a different view of him, however. The
members of this congressional delegation, which visited Georgia in 1979,
were impressed by the Georgian first secretary, finding him outspoken
and free of the rhetoric and dogma so common to Soviet officials.[15] They
had been told by U.S. Embassy officers that Shevardnadze was not well-

informed, and they were surprised by the depth of his presentation. He spoke out strongly on two issues: the arms race, which he condemned as senseless, and China, which he criticized strongly. He complained about the level of military spending, asserted that nuclear weapons were irrational, and denounced the Chinese for their invasion of Vietnam.

The conventional wisdom in the United States and Europe was that because Shevardnadze was "virtually a blank slate in foreign affairs" Gorbachev would be totally in command of foreign policy and thus his own foreign minister.[16] The community of Sovietologists in Washington—particularly Jerry Hough of the Brookings Institution, Dmitri Simes of Johns Hopkins University, and experts at the State Department—concluded that Gorbachev had picked a "new foreign minister cut from his own mold, a man of political wit who will allow Gorbachev to shape his own foreign policy over the long term."[17]

The reaction among Soviet citizens was not favorable, particularly among Russians who believed the foreign minister should be Russian.[18] Shevardnadze's strong Georgian accent was viewed as a particularly serious flaw, and his background in internal security was considered inappropriate for the foreign ministry.[19] The foreign ministry elite certainly would have preferred the selection of one of their own, such as First Deputy Foreign Minister Georgy Korniyenko, a highly respected professional, or Anatoly Dobrynin, longtime Ambassador to the United States. Over time, both men became strong critics of Shevardnadze and his policies, with Korniyenko, in particular, maligning the foreign minister for his lack of credentials.[20] Many foreign policy professionals did not take the appointment seriously, believing Shevardnadze would prove to be only a temporary choice or a figurehead for Gorbachev. The view of some professionals was illustrated in a toast given by a high-ranking diplomat during a visit to Europe in 1986. He raised his glass in a toast to "my Foreign Minister and I mean Foreign Minister Gromyko."[21]

Gorbachev told Shevardnadze that Gromyko, who was named to the figurehead position of Soviet President, had approved of Shevardnadze as a successor. In fact, Gromyko favored one of his own protégés, such as Korniyenko or Dobrynin; according to Gorbachev, Gromyko was "close to shock" when Shevardnadze's name was mentioned.[22] Gromyko, who was being removed from the job he had held since 1957, would have preferred not to go at all, but may have hoped that his replacement by a novice would enable him to continue to manage Soviet foreign policy. Indeed, when Soviet ambassadors returned from assignment abroad early in Shevardnadze's tenure to brief the leadership, including Gorbachev, Gromyko, and the new foreign minister, they felt Gromyko still was playing the dominant role in foreign policy.[23]

Gorbachev defended his appointment of a non-Russian to the foreign ministry, saying that Shevardnadze was, after all, a "Soviet man." As for his lack of experience, Gorbachev remarked: "Well, perhaps that's a good thing. Our foreign policy needs a fresh eye, courage, dynamism, innovative approaches. I have no doubt that my choice is right."[24] Gorbachev believed that the foreign ministry needed an outsider, untainted by old thinking and unconstrained by bureaucratic baggage, if the Soviet Union were to change direction. He knew that Shevardnadze could be counted on to follow a new course with enthusiasm and creativity.

The selection of a Georgian was not altogether surprising, given Georgian loyalty to the Russian, and later Soviet, state for more than 200 years. The Georgians had been loyal to Moscow in the Russo-Turkish war of 1876–77 and had played a major role in the Bolshevik Revolution. There were many Georgians in Lenin's retinue and security guard, and more than 200,000 Georgians were killed in World War II, an extremely large sacrifice for this relatively small republic.

Only one Russian commentator, Zhores Medvedev, argued that Gorbachev had found the perfect man for the job, a man who thought as he did and who understood what needed to be done.[25] Medvedev contended that Shevardnadze's speeches were the only ones worth reading during the early days of Gorbachev's tenure, and he described the new foreign minister as bright, flexible, and an "excellent advocate of the Soviet system." He acknowledged, however, that the appointment was not a popular one among the Russian intelligentsia, who did not need to be reminded that both Stalin and Stalin's murderous police chief, Lavrenti Beria, had been Georgians.[26] One American reporter, Gary Thatcher, did not go along with the pack. He soon nicknamed Shevardnadze "Easy Ed" and speculated that the appointment might signify a new effort to project a "more open public image" to the world.[27]

More important, Secretary of State George Shultz was open-minded and favorably inclined toward his new counterpart. He soon learned that, in Shevardnadze, Gorbachev got a talented politician capable of building personal relationships with foreign leaders while persuasively conveying the new spirit that Gorbachev wanted to promote.

FOREIGN MINISTRY YEARS, 1985–1990

Shevardnadze's tenure as foreign minister can be divided into three phases. The first, a learning phase, lasted until late 1985. Gromyko remained involved in foreign policy, Korniyenko played a major role in running the foreign ministry, and Shevardnadze was a student. The foreign ministry was the major challenge of his life, and he wanted to learn before he acted. During this period, he and Gorbachev met frequently and began to formulate the strategy they would employ to advance their policy of "new thinking." Throughout the second phase, early 1986 through late 1989, Shevardnadze was in charge of the foreign ministry and, increasingly, of foreign policy. With Gorbachev's cooperation and support, he took the lead in formulating and implementing foreign policy initiatives. During this period, the two men worked together extremely well and spoke to each other freely and often. The third phase, December 1989 through December 1990, was a period of increasing friction. Differences began to accumulate and their relationship deteriorated. Toward the end, Gorbachev began to distance himself from Shevardnadze's foreign policy initiatives.

Learning on the Job (1985)

The move to Moscow in 1985 was stressful to Shevardnadze, who looked tired, pale, and even apprehensive during his early months there. He brought much of his Georgian heritage with him and filled his apartment with Georgian furniture, rugs, and art, according to U.S. Secretary of State James Baker, who visited him there in 1989.[28] His security detail was led by an official from Georgia, KGB Major Dmitry Kazachkin, whose father had been a counterintelligence official in the Caucasus. Another official from Georgia, Merabi Chiboshvili, was responsible for Nanuli Shevardnadze's security. Shevardnadze wanted few Georgians in the foreign ministry or his security force because he wanted to display loyalty to the Kremlin and not favoritism to Georgia.

Shevardnadze's inexperience and dependence on the foreign policy bureaucracy were apparent during the first months of his tenure. He brought with him to the foreign ministry only one man, Teimuraz Mamaladze-Stepanov, a longtime aide and the director of the Georgian

Telegraph Agency who was familiar with the pace and style of Shevardnadze's speeches. The two of them had virtually no contacts within the
Moscow establishment.[29] Stepanov was a gifted journalist and writer; he
was never happy in Moscow, where he lacked the perquisites and
amenities of life in Tbilisi. His health was bad, and he soon became
known in the foreign ministry as a malcontent. Nonetheless, he remained
with Shevardnadze throughout the foreign ministry years, wrote Shevardnadze's memoirs in 1991, and returned with him to Tbilisi in 1992.

When Shevardnadze arrived at the foreign ministry, Sergey Tarasenko,
a career diplomat, was assigned as his aide. Tarasenko became very
popular in Washington, where he developed close relations with Baker's
most important aides, Dennis Ross and Robert Zoellick. Tarasenko was
named head of the policy planning department in the foreign ministry in
1987; he remained close to Shevardnadze throughout the foreign ministry
years and accompanied him to Georgia in 1992. However, he was not
Georgian and he felt uncomfortable in Tbilisi; after only six months he
returned to Moscow. Because of Shevardnadze's unpopularity in Russia,
Tarasenko could not get an appointment at the Russian foreign ministry.
He had sacrificed his career for Shevardnadze's policies.

In the beginning, Shevardnadze did not even chair meetings of the
foreign ministry collegium (Korniyenko chaired them), presumably because he did not want to show his inexperience.[30] During his first visit to
the United States, in September 1985, he depended on the advice
of Korniyenko and other members of the so-called American Mafia,
particularly Dobrynin. He made no move to replace these men in the
first stage of his tenure; rather, he relied on them and learned from them.

Secretary of State Shultz has stated that, during his first meeting with
Shevardnadze, in Helsinki in July 1985, Shevardnadze used a prepared
text for his remarks—the only time in thirty such meetings that Shevardnadze stuck to written talking points. He deferred frequently to the
experts who were with him, and they seemed to feel no hesitancy in
responding to questions—particularly those in English, which Shevardnadze did not speak or understand.[31]

Shevardnadze knew he was isolated at the foreign ministry, according
to Tarasenko, and wanted access to what people were thinking and
saying. He believed that everyone would "play the game" and would be
careful not to criticize him or his policies directly, so he used Tarasenko
and Stepanov to gather information for him.[32] While putting in long

days at the ministry, he also took time to travel around the Russian republic to meet with local government and party officials.[33]

During these early months, Shevardnadze demonstrated his ability to work hard and to plan a conceptual framework for what he wanted to accomplish. He refused to act until he understood the details and knew how to accomplish what he wanted, but from the start he indicated there would be changes in approach and that the foreign ministry would become more "open." To Tarasenko and Stepanov, he stressed that it was important to move gradually in order to gain the loyalty of the foreign ministry, where he anticipated resistance to reform and policy changes.[34]

Shevardnadze quickly changed the environment in the ministry, which increased his popularity. Ministry professionals gained additional working space and salary increases. At the same time, he worked seven days a week, sixteen- to eighteen-hour days, and lost twenty-five pounds in several months. All senior members of the ministry felt they also had to work harder too, according to Ambassador Israelyan, but they did so only grudgingly.[35]

An energetic and personable politician rather than a cautious diplomat, Shevardnadze was completely different from Gromyko. Latin American expert Sergo Mikoyan, son of Stalin crony Anastas Mikoyan, described Gromyko as a man who would "rather do nothing than risk making a mistake" and indicated that Shevardnadze was a "breath of fresh air."[36] Korniyenko, a Gromyko protégé, praised his mentor as a man who "listened to the experts" and criticized Shevardnadze as too willing to move ahead without stopping to take expert advice.[37]

Shevardnadze also changed the image of the foreign ministry, which the general public had viewed as elite and aloof. He gave regular interviews and press conferences, and he encouraged his professional staff to meet with the public and the intelligentsia. He established an academic council of experts, including Georgy Arbatov of the Institute of the USA and Canada and Yevgeny Primakov of the Institute of World Economy and International Relations (IMEMO). The ministry sponsored many academic conferences, and Shevardnadze always made himself available to give a keynote speech.[38]

Shevardnadze studied, observed, and learned. Inquisitive by nature, he brought a fresh outsider's view to a stodgy bureaucracy, forcing people to challenge old ideas and assumptions. He was extremely attentive to details and became fascinated with the technical aspects of issues; in this, he differed significantly from Gromyko, who preferred to deal with issues only on a broader level.[39] He took time to walk around the ministry, meeting with people in one-on-one sessions and taking notes of their conversations—again differing from Gromyko, who remained aloof from his staff. By chatting with people over a cup of coffee, Shevardnadze learned who shared his vision of the world and who would work easily with him. He was eager for new ideas and prepared to forward them to Gorbachev.

Shevardnadze learned immediately that the key issue was arms control and understood that significant changes had to be made in the Soviet approach. He had a vision of where he wanted to go but lacked command of the substantive details. The foreign minister knew that he would have to fight the military on disarmament, particularly the instructions for nuclear weapons negotiations. He and Gorbachev began to work in tandem to overcome the objections of military and conservative party figures and to push their new vision of the world and of foreign policy.

Taking Charge, 1986

The end of Shevardnadze's "learning" phase was marked by a series of definite events. The first, in November 1985, was his chairing of a foreign ministry collegium meeting; from that time on, he was totally in charge of these meetings. The second occurred in May 1986, when Gorbachev made an unprecedented and dramatic appearance at a meeting of the foreign ministry staff. According to Tarasenko, the foreign minister had solicited this appearance.[40] In his speech, Gorbachev emphatically and enthusiastically endorsed Shevardnadze as foreign minister, thus putting an end to continuing rumors that Shevardnadze's tenure would be brief. He also demanded that the "form and content" of diplomacy be "modernized" and warned that the Central Committee would "strictly monitor" the progress of reorganization.[41]

Shevardnadze used Gorbachev's endorsement to restructure the foreign ministry, getting rid of the old elite as well as their relatives and protégés and installing his own deputies.[42] A major change was pushing out Dobrynin, who had been an obvious choice to succeed Gromyko as foreign minister. Far more experienced and knowledgeable than Shevardnadze, he was particularly skilled in the critical area of relations with Washington, where he had served for nearly twenty-five years. Dobrynin was called back to Moscow in 1986 to run the Central Committee's International Department, thus removing him from the foreign ministry. Shevardnadze presumably had advocated the removal of his rival from the ministry.

As he gained confidence, Shevardnadze moved vigorously to energize the foreign policy bureaucracy. On every foreign trip he spoke to the diplomatic corps. He described his strong interest in literature, theater, and cinema, and he urged diplomats to take advantage of their own unique areas of interest and expertise. He introduced competitions for young diplomats that required essays suggesting innovation and reform. In this way, he promoted outstanding young officers—and encouraged change.[43]

By the summer of 1986, Shevardnadze had made significant changes in the ministry. There were more personnel changes than in any other government ministry, more women were inducted into the foreign ministry, and an Information Department was created to emphasize public diplomacy. He tried to end the traditional practice of nepotism in the ministry, but the practice had become so entrenched that it was difficult to change it significantly. His son, Pata, for example, was a UNESCO official in Paris.

Shevardnadze used his influence with Gorbachev to weaken the positions of those whose views were different from his. The new foreign minister did this by becoming an expert himself, particularly in the arcane field of arms control. Shevardnadze's victory was complete in October 1988, when both Gromyko and Dobrynin were sent into retirement. By that time, there was really only one man driving policy and that was Shevardnadze. Gorbachev, whose focus was domestic reform, did not, in fact, want to run his own foreign policy.[44]

Having removed his rivals and established his authority, Shevardnadze used his political skills to further his own independence. Gorbachev had weakened the central institutions of power (the Politburo and the Party) so Shevardnadze began to short-circuit normal procedures. It was standard practice, for example, for Politburo members to submit drafts of speeches to their colleagues far enough ahead of time to permit review and revision. Shevardnadze circulated his drafts immediately before delivery so that no one had time to interfere.[45]

In dealing with Gorbachev during this period, Shevardnadze was patient and low-key. Typically, the Politburo would meet as a whole, then a smaller group would meet, then Gorbachev and Shevardnadze would meet alone. Shevardnadze would not speak in the larger meetings except on matters of foreign policy. He used his one-on-one sessions with Gorbachev, however, to make his points on everything; during this phase, according to Tarasenko, Gorbachev tended to follow Shevardnadze's advice.[46]

Shevardnadze also manipulated the system in reverse. He would first speak privately with Gorbachev, encouraging him to make a particular point or state a particular principle in a speech. He would then take Gorbachev's statements and use them to argue with others that this was what the general secretary wanted. He used such tactics to advance policy in spite of serious opposition, particularly from the military. He was not dishonest, in Tarasenko's view, but he was highly political and did not always approach things directly.[47] At the same time, Shevardnadze was careful to avoid provoking Gorbachev's ire by being willing to stand in the shadows and not take credit for his ideas and policies. Ever mindful of the political game, he gave the credit to Gorbachev, who was as eager to take it as Shevardnadze was to give it to him.

Throughout this second phase, Shevardnadze and Gorbachev stood together against conservative challenges within the party hierarchy. Shevardnadze was staunch in his support of Gorbachev's leadership position, particularly in October 1987, when Boris Yeltsin launched his attack on Yegor Ligachev (and, by implication, Gorbachev) for not proceeding rapidly enough with reform. Gorbachev, Yakovlev, and Shevardnadze came to the defense of Ligachev, whose support they believed they needed to achieve domestic change. Consistent with his past history, Shevardnadze was effusive in his praise for Ligachev, calling him, "a man of the highest moral principles, committed, as they say, body and soul to the business of perestroika." And he denounced Yeltsin, calling his speech a "betrayal of the party."[48] Shevardnadze's harsh criticism of Yeltsin initiated what would prove to be continuing friction between these two men. Yeltsin became hostile to Shevardnadze and to the foreign ministry because of this episode; the two men were not even on speaking terms for several years.

When the Gorbachev-Ligachev struggle for power became intense, Shevardnadze and Ligachev became embroiled in their own ideological war. In an extraordinary speech to the foreign ministry in July 1988, Shevardnadze openly attacked what had been a basic assumption of Soviet foreign policy. He stated that ideology should no longer be the basis of foreign policy, and he disavowed any connection between foreign policy and the class struggle. The following month, Ligachev explicitly defended the principle Shevardnadze had rejected, insisting that class struggle must be the basis of all Soviet policy, both domestic and foreign.[49] The struggle between Shevardnadze and Ligachev over events surrounding the tragic use of force in Tbilisi in April 1989 further exacerbated relations between the two men.

THE RIFT BETWEEN GORBACHEV AND SHEVARDNADZE

Differences between Gorbachev and Shevardnadze began to appear in 1988, but the relationship itself did not begin to deteriorate until 1989, when Shevardnadze became convinced that Gorbachev was moving to the right politically and that, in any event, he had outgrown the president and was ready to proceed with his own agenda. Differences over the Tbilisi tragedy of 1989 contributed to the strains, and by early 1990 every issue had become a struggle, with each fight taking its toll. The two men stopped meeting one-on-one, communication became distant and strained, and they used different language in discussing the underlying assumptions of new thinking in foreign policy.

Gorbachev continued to couch his arguments for a new approach to international relations in the terminology of Marxism-Leninism, in part to appease Ligachev, KGB Chief Vladimir Kryuchkov, and Defense Minister Dmitry Yazov—all opponents of Shevardnadze. He spoke of class struggle, denounced imperialism as the root of militarism and adventurism, and argued that the "prestige and role of socialism in world development" were on the rise.[50] He continued to refer to the "Western military bloc led by the United States," stating that it behaved "with open aggression toward socialism." He referred to new thinking as a dialectical approach that was "in keeping with our socialist choice, our Leninist principles."[51]

In June 1988, the month before Shevardnadze's speech to the foreign ministry asserting that class struggle was no longer the basis for understanding international relations, Gorbachev had told the 19th All-Union Party Conference: "international relations, without losing their class nature, are being increasingly realized as relations among people."[52] He argued that the core of new political thinking lay in the Marxist interconnection between proletarian interests and interests common to all humankind.[53]

In contrast, in his speech to the Supreme Soviet in October 1989, Shevardnadze made no reference to socialism or to Marxist-Leninist ideology. He indicated that Soviet policy would be guided not by Leninist norms but by "common human values," and that guidance in this regard is provided by "generally recognized documents, primarily the U.N. Charter and the declarations, pacts, conventions, and resolutions adopted and observed by the overwhelming majority of world states."[54] Thus, while Gorbachev remained bound by "old thinking," Shevardnadze had become more secular and international in his outlook. The outcome was inevitable: while Shevardnadze was ready to move forward with reform quickly, Gorbachev vacillated and refused to take the political risks necessary to move ahead.

Violence in Tbilisi

The relationship between Gorbachev and Shevardnadze, already severely strained, never recovered from the killing of demonstrators in Tbilisi in April 1989. At that time, Georgian nationalists were demanding Georgian secession from the Soviet Union; the Abkhaz minority, in turn, was demanding secession from Georgia. Thousands of people gathered outside government offices in Tbilisi, leading to an attack by Soviet troops on April 9 that resulted in nineteen deaths. The journal *Ogonek*, edited by Vitaly Korotich, an ally of Shevardnadze's, pointed an accusatory finger at Ligachev, indicating that he had chaired the Politburo meeting at which the decision to send troops into the city (resulting in the use of force) had been made.[55]

Ligachev insisted that a decision to send Shevardnadze to Georgia to head off trouble had been made by the Politburo at an airport meeting on the evening of April 7, with both Gorbachev and Shevardnadze present. He accused Shevardnadze of failing to follow Gorbachev's order to fly to Tbilisi immediately and seek a peaceful solution to the crisis.[56] Shevardnadze disputed Ligachev's version, claiming that no meeting was held and that no polling of the Politburo had occurred.[57]

The aftermath of the Georgian tragedy was a political disaster. Shevardnadze, party official Georgy Razumovsky, and Tarasenko went to Tbilisi immediately after the shootings to investigate the episode. They concluded that the military had made many mistakes—but due to ineptitude, not malice or intent. A Supreme Soviet commission headed by Leningrad Mayor Anatoly Sobchak subsequently prepared a report that drew similar conclusions.

Shevardnadze believed there was high-level agreement that the report of the Sobchak commission would be delivered to the Soviet Congress of People's Deputies and that no debate would be permitted. When the report was presented on December 24, 1989, however, it drew an immediate, negative response from the military, which presented a dissenting report strongly defending the military's actions and blaming the victims for having provoked the tragedy. This speech received an enthusiastic response from the deputies. During the break, Shevardnadze asked to be given the floor to respond, but Gorbachev refused to let him speak.[58]

Gorbachev almost certainly had approved the preparation and presentation of the second report—without telling Shevardnadze.[59] This approval, and Gorbachev's rejection of Shevardnadze's request to speak to the Congress, was the first outward manifestation of the disintegration of the relationship between Gorbachev and Shevardnadze and the first clear demonstration of Gorbachev's siding with the military against Shevardnadze. Shevardnadze seriously considered resigning after this episode: "I felt I had to resign since we had an agreement: to listen to Sobchak's report and not open discussions. Suddenly the floor was turned over to the procurator and it was all a pack of lies."[60]

Accumulating Differences

Numerous differences on matters of policy developed between Gorbachev and Shevardnadze during the next twelve months. The most important involved Gorbachev's gestures to the military. In November 1990, Gorbachev sponsored a series of steps to appease the military, including measures to allow soldiers to defend themselves and their interests with weapons against "nationalists." This was clearly in response to hostile behavior toward Soviet troops in the Baltics. Also in November 1990, Gorbachev allowed the Soviet military to move more than 16,000 tanks east of the Urals to avoid having to destroy them under the terms of the Conventional Forces in Europe (CFE) treaty—but Shevardnadze apparently was not informed. He was caught off guard and embarrassed during negotiations with the United States.[61] Finally, Gorbachev failed to defend Shevardnadze when the military attacked him for his role in agreeing to German reunification.

There also were policy differences between Gorbachev and Shevardnadze on Third World issues. Shevardnadze was actively involved in international negotiations for a settlement in Cambodia. He had urged the Cambodian government to compromise, criticized the Khmer Rouge for boycotting the negotiating process, and issued a joint statement with the Chinese promising not to arm Cambodian factions. In late 1990, however, when the Cambodian government rejected key provisions of the peace plan, the Soviets implicitly endorsed its recalcitrance; this vacillation suggested that Shevardnadze's approach was being challenged.[62] With respect to South Korea, increasing ambivalence within the Soviet leadership was evident. Moscow was moving toward establishing diplomatic ties with Seoul at Shevardnadze's urging, but Gorbachev's meeting with South Korean President No Tae-U in San Francisco in June 1990 was played down in the Soviet press. Yevgeny Primakov, an adviser to Gorbachev, had accompanied the president and had indicated that he favored slowing the pace of relations. When Shevardnadze met with the South Koreans in New York in September, he preempted Primakov and immediately established relations.[63]

In July 1990, two months before Shevardnadze's third visit to Japan, Soviet Vice President Gennady Yanayev was named party leader in charge of Soviet diplomacy toward Japan—a clear slap at Shevardnadze. During his visit to Tokyo in September, Shevardnadze indicated willingness to negotiate the territorial dispute over the Northern Territories with Japan. A month later, Yanayev visited Tokyo and repeated the old intransigent Soviet position.[64] But differences were most dramatically revealed during the Persian Gulf crisis, when Yevgeny Primakov visited Iraq without Shevardnadze's approval. While Shevardnadze emphasized cooperation with the West even if it meant sanctioning the use of force, Gorbachev and Primakov wanted more time to pursue a negotiated solution.

Shevardnadze's Resignation

During the Houston ministerial meeting in December 1990, Shevardnadze was unable to gain Gorbachev's support for a position he was advocating. He was not aware that the Soviet military had redesignated armed units as naval infantry and had moved armor and artillery behind the Urals, violating the spirit of the CFE treaty. When Gorbachev expressed the view that these movements were not significant, Shevardnadze privately vented his frustration, stating, "I can't take this anymore!"[65]

Upon returning to Moscow, Shevardnadze was called before parliament to report on foreign policy. He was under severe attack by military critics at this time and felt that he did not have Gorbachev's support. Early in the morning of the day he was scheduled to appear, he met with his aides, Tarasenko and Stepanov, and informed them that he planned to resign. They agreed with the decision. Shevardnadze called his wife and children, all of whom also agreed. Tarasenko advised him not to inform Gorbachev ahead of time, as Gorbachev would press Shevardnadze to stay, putting the foreign minister in an awkward position.[66] Shevardnadze agreed, and Gorbachev got no advance warning of his resignation.

Shevardnadze later described his resignation as "an act of disagreement and protest, and simultaneously a warning." He said he had told Gorbachev he understood the complexity of the president's position, but that the political situation in Moscow was becoming critical. He also recognized that Gorbachev had to make choices and that some decisions would not be to Shevardnadze's liking. At the same time, he did not believe he should openly oppose Gorbachev, because "Gorbachev personified perestroika and to oppose any of his decisions would be to oppose perestroika."[67]

Developments at the 28th Party Congress in July 1990 should have alerted Gorbachev to the dangers that lay ahead, in Shevardnadze's view. He argued that the alignment of forces and the atmosphere at the congress demonstrated that those who wanted to stop reform were in the ascendancy, and this in turn suggested that "the president was already doing something wrong." He and Gorbachev had talked "fairly candidly," Shevardnadze said, and he had tried to warn Gorbachev about the increasing force of nationalism and the dangers of resorting to force. "When I began to suspect that there was some trouble involving the Baltics, I called him on his car phone" to tell him that the use of force in the Baltics would mean catastrophe. "Is it really possible? . . . After Tbilisi, after all the other well-known events?" Gorbachev answered "categorically" that such an approach had been ruled out, and Shevardnadze believed him. Shevardnadze subsequently held firm to his belief that Gorbachev did not know the military was planning to use force in Lithuania.[68]

In his own view, Shevardnadze was not deserting his friend by resigning. He has maintained that the resignation was designed to save their common cause by shocking Gorbachev into recognizing the dangerous situation and taking action. He hoped to force Gorbachev to face reality.[69] When Gorbachev came to the foreign ministry in January 1991 to install Alexander Bessmertnykh as the new minister, however, he presented his own version of events, recounting his feelings of betrayal when Shevardnadze resigned and stating that he would never forgive Shevardnadze for not consulting him beforehand.[70] That was particularly painful, he said, because Shevardnadze had always been "by my side, my closest comrade in all the most difficult situations and, most important, in making the choice."[71]

Shevardnadze agreed with Gorbachev that making "the choice" had been the most important thing—the choice of "a path, a line of behavior, an ally, a friend." But, he said, there are limits to such choices: "You choose but also are chosen, and if the choices coincide everything is fine. If they do not, then you must make another choice."[72]

Reprise

After the failed coup against Gorbachev in August 1991, Bessmertnykh was removed as foreign minister because of his failure to oppose the coup leaders and defend Gorbachev. Boris Pankin, the ambassador to Czechoslovakia who refused to pass on foreign ministry instructions announcing the takeover by the coup leaders, became foreign minister. He was not capable of performing the functions of the job, however, and, in November 1991 Shevardnadze returned to the foreign ministry. The officers of the Soviet foreign ministry circulated a petition calling for Shevardnadze's return as foreign minister; all but thirteen of the 3,000 officers signed the petition. Although he was realistic about the problems he faced and about the prognosis for the country, he felt he had to go back. His return was short-lived; the Soviet Union collapsed in December.

RETROSPECTIVE

Before the stewardship of Gorbachev and Shevardnadze, Moscow had relied on three sets of expectations: that the Soviet bloc would grow in strength and influence, that the capitalist West and Japan would face a series of economic and political crises, and that the Third World would move into the Soviet orbit. Even before Gorbachev's and Shevardnadze's accession to power in 1985, it was obvious that none of those expectations would come true. These two men had come to realize this, but their predecessors, old Bolsheviks, had not. They had ignored both the impact of the Sino-Soviet split in the late 1950s and the tensions in Eastern Europe in the 1960s and 1970s—particularly the invasion of Czechoslovakia in 1968, which undermined Moscow's position in Europe and Asia. International communism, in fact, ceased to exist as a movement, but Moscow's national security system continued to act as if the Kremlin still had strong cards to play in the world arena. In truth, Moscow's economic and technological backwardness meant that it was playing with an increasingly weak hand.

Gromyko, Dobrynin, and Korniyenko continued to boast of a "positive correlation of force" for Soviet diplomacy, but Gorbachev and Shevardnadze understood that Moscow had become increasingly isolated in the world arena and that its military power had not bought geopolitical success. They did not continue the efforts of their predecessors to promote the control and integration of Eastern Europe under Soviet auspices, and they were out in front in realizing the need to pursue economic and technological cooperation with the West. Moscow's leaders understood that the Kremlin would have to get its domestic house in order before it could assert itself abroad. Shevardnadze told a foreign ministry audience in 1986 that the "key to success in foreign policy lies in reliability and solidarity on the home front, . . . in the healthy conditions of Soviet society and economy."[73]

Asked how it was that he and Gorbachev had lost out to "mediocrities" when they had possessed so much intellect, energy, and will, Shevardnadze conceded that they had made mistakes. They had had a sense of where they had to go, but "society was not ready and we were not ready and the party was not ready," particularly the Politburo. He cited one mistake in particular: the failure to take advantage of Gorbachev's influence and popularity during the first years of perestroika to "force the old system in a new way, . . . to use it to greater effect—until the new one started to work."[74] Alexander Yakovlev said the chief mistake the leaders of perestroika had made was to think it was possible to reform the ruling system. Eventually, it became clear that the system simply would not accept reform.[75]

The second Soviet revolution that had begun with so much energy, enthusiasm, and conviction ended in bitterness, disappointment, and disillusion. Shevardnadze and Gorbachev had shared a vision of the revitalization of a socialist system that had grown stagnant and corrupt. They had worked together to end the Soviet Union's isolation by ending the Cold War, to lessen the drain on resources generated by an inflated military-industrial complex, and to modernize an economy weighed down by an inefficient, centralized command structure. In the end, the task was too great, and the two old friends came to a parting of the ways. They parted company over the speed and urgency of domestic reform. They had failed to keep pace with their own revolution.

3

DOMESTIC IMPERATIVE

The Need to Reform

> There is no sense in de-
> fending a system that has
> led to economic and social
> dislocation. There is only
> one solution: politics must
> take on the task of creating
> a reserve of security while
> cutting spending on arms.
> —Eduard Shevardnadze

When Gorbachev and Shevardnadze agreed that the Soviet system was rotten, they were focusing on the domestic situation, particularly the decadent political and economic structures. They clearly understood that the Soviet Union's heavy military burden, driven by its competition with the United States, was preventing essential investment in the domestic economy and contributing to stagnation and decay. They recognized that tense relations with the United States, exacerbated by aggressive Soviet actions in the Third World, were inhibiting progress toward arms control. Shortly after the Soviet invasion of Afghanistan in December 1979, the two men met and agreed that the invasion was a fatal error that would cost the country dearly. According to Shevardnadze, "It was clear to us that if we did not change our foreign policy by removing the main sources of distrust—the use of force and rigid ideology—we would never create a zone of security around our country."[1]

Recognition that the Soviet Union's security could best be served by improving relations with the West, thereby easing pressure to increase military spending and permitting serious efforts to deal with domestic problems, was at the heart of new political thinking. The tight linkage of domestic and foreign policies was the major theoretical contribution Gorbachev, Shevardnadze, and Alexander Yakovlev made. The three men agreed that the most serious problem facing them was economic and that revitalizing the economy superseded any possible military threat. As they focused on possible solutions, they came to believe that Moscow's foreign policy would have to change profoundly to permit domestic reform. Shevardnadze explained: "It is not only impossible but also extremely dangerous to divide domestic from foreign policy. The notion that we can ignore the world around us and disregard other peoples' interests has cost our people and socialism dearly in the past. One of the foundations of new political thinking is the understanding of the high degree of unity and interdependence of the modern world."[2]

A fundamental revision of foreign policy was essential to success in restructuring the economy (perestroika). New thinking required a redefinition of the priorities of a foreign policy that had produced a costly arms competition, undermined economic progress, produced a series of foreign policy blunders, and resulted in Moscow's isolation from the international community. The new leaders would seek to improve Moscow's relations with the United States, promote international stability, and gain access to Western investment and technology. Becoming a full member of the international community would give the Soviet Union the time and resources needed to improve its domestic situation. Thus, the domestic imperative would drive foreign policy, while foreign policy would provide the breathing space necessary for domestic revitalization.

Shevardnadze, along with Gorbachev and Yakovlev, believed that national security derived from a healthy, dynamic economy, not from military power—a sharp break from traditional Soviet thinking. He believed in the "organic connection" between the major changes taking place in the socialist community and the world at large, and understood that the Soviet Union had been isolated from many of these changes.[3] He argued that the "goal of diplomacy was to form an external environment favorable for internal development."[4] Inertia in our thinking, he said, can block realization that the world is "rapidly changing before our very eyes" and that many traditional views, "possibly correct" in the past, are now "hopelessly outdated."[5]

OUT OF ISOLATION TOWARD A NEW WORLD ORDER

In his speech to the United Nations in December 1988, Gorbachev coined a phrase that was to have considerable resonance in the post–Cold War era, and that was subsequently attributed incorrectly to President George Bush. He declared that further world progress would be possible only if there were progress toward creation of "a new world order."[6] Shevardnadze became the most vocal and consistent proponent of the new Soviet goal of redefining the international environment and creating this new world order.

Moscow's drive for military parity with the United States, its active support for anti-U.S. forces in the Third World, and its view of two conflicting world systems had isolated the Soviet Union and its allies. The socialist countries did not experience the economic expansion of the Western world and even lagged behind many countries in the developing world, particularly those in Asia. The costs of superpower status, an expanding empire, and self-imposed isolation had become an impossible burden. Shevardnadze was convinced that a radical change in Moscow's international position was essential.

Gorbachev, Shevardnadze, and Yakovlev certainly did not anticipate the enormous extent of the impact their policies would have on the international system—that they would, in fact, precipitate the collapse of the postwar order. Their fundamental motive for pursuing domestic reform was to preserve socialism, and their motive for changing foreign policy was to redefine and strengthen Moscow's position in the international system. Shevardnadze would later claim that he had anticipated the revolutions in Eastern Europe and the reunification of Germany, but it is more likely that he rationalized many of the consequences of "new thinking" and developed creative ideas for coping with new realities. He certainly did not anticipate the collapse of communism in Eastern Europe, of the Warsaw Pact, and, eventually, of the Soviet Union itself.

ECONOMIC AND POLITICAL INHERITANCE

Economic stagnation had been a cause for concern since the 1950s, when Nikita Khrushchev had tried and failed to implement reform. Stagnation was reflected in declining productivity, increasing grain imports, aging capital stock, hard-currency shortfalls, lagging oil production, and the inability to keep pace with scientific and technological developments in the West. The rate of annual growth had been declining since the late 1960s, and by the time Gorbachev came to power the economy had been experiencing a decade-long slump, averaging just over 2 percent growth a year.[7]

Of greater concern were trends indicating that economic performance would become even worse in the future. These included long-term decline in capital and labor productivity, decay of the economic and social infrastructure, growth in public consumption exceeding economic growth, and an expanding technological gap between the West and the Soviet Union. Moscow also faced the prospect of declining oil exports, its major source of hard currency. The Soviet Union is rich in natural resources, but these resources have been squandered because "it was always assumed that there would be new deposits over the horizon whenever the existing deposits were depleted."[8] The Soviet Union had been a major exporter of petroleum in the 1970s and 1980s, but by the late 1980s the oil industry was faced with a crisis brought on by "inefficiency and low productivity, poor organization and technological backwardness, waste and environmental neglect."[9] In short, the oil industry was facing problems similar to those of the rest of the Soviet economy.

The policies of the Brezhnev regime had disastrous consequences. Massive protectionism of major economic and institutional interests, particularly those of the military and its supportive industrial complex, had generated powerful but inefficient ministries, rigid investment priorities, and a ruling class that based its legitimacy not on enhancing economic performance but on buying public support. With a deteriorating economic base and inferior computer-based information-processing and communications systems, Moscow faced erosion of the military parity it had struggled so hard to achieve.

The Soviet Union was not even keeping pace in the field to which it had devoted its greatest resources: military technology and production. In response to the USSR's deployment of SS-20 missiles during the 1970s, Western European nations had accepted deployment of U.S. short-range cruise and Pershing II nuclear missiles on their territory and were accelerating force modernization. The United States, under Presidents Jimmy Carter and Ronald Reagan, had increased military spending and was pressing forward with plans for new strategic weaponry and a 600-ship naval force. U.S. plans to proceed with the Strategic Defense Initiative (SDI) for weapons in outer space threatened to destabilize the strategic balance and force Soviet military planners to spend substantial resources developing a counter. Technological spinoffs of SDI, including deep penetration weapons systems, further threatened Soviet forces in Europe. The development of Stealth technology for aircraft and cruise missiles raised yet another challenge to Soviet air defenses.

The political structure was similarly stagnant. The ruling elite had become aged and morally bankrupt. Lower-level officials, blocked from promotion and frustrated by the unresponsiveness of the system, often turned to corruption—both for their own enrichment and to make the system work. Economic and political stagnation had contributed to increasing domestic cynicism, evident in widespread corruption, alcoholism, and job absenteeism. Ironically, as individuals within the system came to measure success in terms of their own short-term economic gains, the economy was becoming increasingly unable to satisfy their demands.

Yury Andropov, who succeeded Brezhnev as general secretary in November 1982, represented the Soviet leaders who considered it their primary task to get the country moving again by increasing the efficiency of the existing system. During his short tenure, Andropov authorized Nikolay Ryzhkov, who later became prime minister, to sponsor a series of studies to investigate major problems, particularly economic, facing the country. (Gorbachev later said that there were more than one hundred such studies and that they had created the basis for perestroika.[10]) Andropov's policy initiatives during his short tenure were designed to raise productivity, reduce corruption, tighten discipline in the workplace, and stimulate the party apparatus to improve its performance. While these policies were the precursors of Gorbachev's reforms, they actually did little to improve the situation and provided warning that incremental measures would have only limited impact on the nation's problems.

INTERNATIONAL LEGACY

Moscow's international position in 1985 was no more promising than its domestic position. Every important bilateral relationship was at an impasse or in disarray. U.S.-Soviet arms control talks were nonexistent following Moscow's abrupt departure from both the Strategic Arms Reduction Talks (START) and the Intermediate-range Nuclear Forces (INF) negotiations. The ideological opposition of the United States to dealing with the Soviet Union had reached its apex. Soviet relations with China were stagnant, and Foreign Minister Gromyko's hostility toward Japan hampered development of relations with Tokyo. In Western Europe, where many nations had become more conservative and less willing to pursue close relations with Moscow, Soviet prospects also were in decline.[11]

Eastern Europe had become a significant burden on the Soviet Union. If the purpose of empire is to maximize the imperial state's economic growth, security, and international influence, then Moscow's empire in Eastern Europe was a failure, generating fewer and fewer returns. Extensive trade subsidies, the burden of maintaining military forces throughout the region, recurring economic crises, and Eastern Europe's resistance to Soviet pressure to reform increased the costs to the USSR. Soviet involvement in Eastern Europe undercut political stability in the USSR by increasing the dissatisfaction of Soviet citizens who knew that the quality of life was higher in Eastern Europe. There were also international costs. The growing tendency of Eastern European states to disregard Soviet decisions, and the obvious economic and political problems of the socialist countries, made Third World states question the utility of either adopting the Soviet model or becoming dependent on the Soviet Union.

The Soviet position in the Third World was no better than elsewhere. While many Western observers argued that the Soviet position was improving and that its policy remained robust and expansionist, the truth was that Moscow's global position was weak. The USSR had made no gains in the Far East commensurate with its large military presence there. The Sino-Soviet dispute convinced key Asian states to keep Moscow at arm's length. Moscow's support for Vietnam's occupation of Cambodia made other, rapidly developing, Southeast Asian states unwilling to improve ties.

Moscow had played no role in the Middle East agreements negotiated from 1974 to 1979 under three American presidents, and the invasion of Afghanistan in 1979 had undermined prospects throughout the Middle East and Southwest Asia. The Soviet position in Africa had peaked in the late 1970s, when Moscow and its Cuban proxy took advantage of openings in Angola and Ethiopia; by 1985 the costs of Soviet involvement were getting greater and the rewards were getting smaller. In Central America, Moscow's modest support for Nicaragua served only to exacerbate its relations with the United States. The insurgency in El Salvador, indirectly backed by the Soviet Union, had done the same.[12] Close Soviet relations with Cuba remained a source of friction between Moscow and Washington.

Finally, Moscow was finding it expensive to prop up its Marxist-Leninist clients in the Third World. Its annual subsidies to Cuba and Vietnam exceeded $5 billion. Prolonged conflicts in client states such as Afghanistan, Angola, Ethiopia, Cambodia, and Nicaragua were a drain on Soviet resources. The Soviet Union had become a status quo power, sustaining some of the more repressive and impoverished regimes in the Third World. Shevardnadze had been dealt an extremely weak international hand.

DOMESTIC LINKS TO FOREIGN POLICY

In debating how to energize the economy, many Soviet commentators had long argued that international policies must be based on realistic appraisals of both the domestic and international situations. Throughout the 1970s, Soviet academics debated international economic trends and drew implications for the Soviet Union. They recognized that the international economy was operating as an interdependent system and that Moscow's vision of separate and opposing capitalist and socialist systems was misguided and counterproductive.[13] They wrote extensively about the internationalization of the world economy, the mutual dependence of countries of different political and social systems, and the interconnections arising from pollution, energy, and oceanic issues. Many of them concluded that growth within the Soviet Union was being retarded by Moscow's exclusion from the world economy.[14]

Shevardnadze and Gorbachev agreed that the Soviets had isolated themselves from key economic developments in Europe. Their numerous conversations in the 1970s had focused on the backwardness of the Soviet economy and the need for growth in industrial technology, particularly in the machine-building sector. Shevardnadze was convinced that the Soviet Union was falling behind every industrial country in the world. As a result, he, even more than Gorbachev, became increasingly committed to economic reform, recognizing that reform was essential to the political stability of the USSR.

Shevardnadze especially deplored the fact that the Soviet Union remained outside the major international economic institutions, not participating in the General Agreement on Tariffs and Trade (GATT) or the International Monetary Fund (IMF). It was isolated from the extensive trading opportunities generated by the rapid scientific and technological progress of the Western world. In a highly interdependent world experiencing revolutions in science, technology, and communications, the USSR was paying a high price for its insularity.

Both Gorbachev and Shevardnadze shared the perceptions of Soviet commentators and academics who believed that domestic restructuring and growth depended upon a revitalization of the Soviet Union's foreign position.[15] Since the Bolshevik Revolution, Moscow's approach to the international system had been shaped by its competition with the West, its commitment to expanding the world socialist system, and its isolation from the global economy. These fundamental assumptions had to change. It would be necessary to forge an economic and political alliance with the West, to move out of the isolated socialist system, and to integrate the USSR into the global system.

Foreign Policy as Locomotive

Economic revitalization at home was Gorbachev's primary objective when he came to power in March 1985. Shevardnadze confirmed that virtually all Soviet leaders agreed that major steps had to be taken to reverse the stagnation of the Brezhnev years and that, for this reason, Gorbachev's accession to power was "inevitable." The problem, however, was that people had very different ideas about how to accomplish change, how far to go, and how quickly to move.

The approach of the new regime had a number of interlocking elements. Economic deregulation, which Shevardnadze had introduced in Georgia, was expected to create the incentives and competition essential to building a more productive economy. Political deregulation was supposed to break the stranglehold of the party and the ministries over the economy. Deregulation of the socialist bloc was expected to ease the external burdens placed on the Soviet economy. Movement toward "democratization" and a "market economy" was expected to produce an economic and political alliance with the West that would reconcile the goals of security, growth, and stability.

Gorbachev and Shevardnadze recognized that transformation of foreign policy would be easier than change at home and hoped that reducing tension in the international environment would provide both breathing room and necessary support for the more difficult and prolonged process of domestic reform. They pushed earlier and more strongly for international change than for political and economic liberalization because they sensed victories would come sooner and would advance domestic reform. Foreign policy would be the locomotive pulling the Soviet Union into the international system and providing the time and energy necessary for economic resurgence.

Strategic Vision or Vacuum?

Shevardnadze's mission at the foreign ministry was to eliminate the ideological assumptions driving foreign policy, to end Moscow's isolation in the international arena, and to improve relations with the United States. Success in these areas would enable Moscow to reduce military spending significantly, thereby easing the burden on the economy. Former Soviet officials have differed on the question of whether Shevardnadze's approach to foreign policy was conceptual and strategic. Sergey Khrushchev, son of the former Soviet leader, has stated that Shevardnadze's policies lacked vision and were unrealistic and emotional; he blames the ultimate collapse of the Soviet Union on the failure of the new leadership to anticipate the results of new political thinking.[16] Ambassador Vladimir Petrovsky, on the other hand, has asserted that Shevardnadze came to the foreign ministry with a clear understanding of Soviet society, a recognition of how closely domestic reform was linked to foreign policy, and the necessary will and energy to move the Soviet Union toward international cooperation.[17]

Tarasenko, Shevardnadze's close adviser, observes that Shevardnadze did not think in strategic terms and did not know where his policies eventually would lead; while he knew there must be radical reform, he did not understand all the implications of that reform. He thought in terms of changing the system and may even have thought in terms of promoting democratic socialism. Tarasenko argues that by the 1980s, not many people explicitly tied reform to socialism or political philosophy of any kind, because few Soviet leaders really cared about that ideological linkage.[18] It seems fair to say that, in keeping with his personality and past approach to political issues, Shevardnadze's approach was pragmatic and adaptive, not bound by a particular political framework. That is not to say, however, that this approach lacked coherence and strategic vision. In fact, new political thinking did have internal consistency, a coherent set of objectives, and a logical framework for action.

Shevardnadze believed that the foreign ministry had to clear the path for domestic reform by changing the international environment, removing obstacles to reform. He knew the Soviet Union must join international financial institutions, become a normal member of the international community, expand its trade relations, eliminate certain burdens, and change its image. He knew that huge military expenses could not be sustained and that fundamental changes to move the country ahead would have to be made. It was all very logical and pragmatic, but it was also inherently radical, even revolutionary, and it would prove extremely destabilizing.

AXIOMS OF NEW POLITICAL THINKING

Shevardnadze may not have come to the foreign ministry with a clearly defined political philosophy and a strategic agenda, and it is clear that he did not know where new political thinking ultimately would lead. But he and Gorbachev certainly developed a framework, a set of assumptions, and a plan of action that were strategic in scope. During his five years as foreign minister, Shevardnadze pursued coherent policies that flowed from clear goals and priorities. Recognizing acute economic problems at home, he required international predictability; to achieve that, he pursued a pragmatic foreign policy that was goal-oriented and strategically unified.

Primacy of Economic Revitalization

New political thinking was based on several key assumptions. The first assumption was the fundamental imperative of reviving the stagnant economy. Gorbachev told the 27th Communist Party Congress in March 1986 that saving an economy in crisis superseded any external military threat as the Soviet Union's "primary task."[19] In a speech in July 1987, Shevardnadze elaborated on the theme that foreign policy must advance economic strength:

> The time has come today to introduce economics into Soviet foreign policy for, until it merges completely with economics, it will not be able to assist in restructuring the Soviet internal economy and society in general . . . , which otherwise will not be able to participate on equal terms in the competitive political struggle for making its social and political model of development attractive.[20]

In a subsequent interview he added: "No less important for national security than the accumulation of arms are the economic price and the profitability of foreign policy."[21]

Need for International Stability

The second assumption of new thinking was that economic revival and the protection of Soviet national security could be achieved only through international stability. Immediately after taking over as foreign minister, Shevardnadze spoke in Helsinki to a session of the Conference on Security and Cooperation in Europe (CSCE) and made the linkage clear: "The foreign policy of any state is inseparably linked to its internal affairs. . . . The Soviet Union needs a durable peace."[22]

For the stability he sought, it would be necessary to reduce East-West tensions, lessen the costs of competing in a "no-win" arms race, and create a more relaxed international environment in order to enhance the prospects of gaining increased credits and trade with the West. Speaking to foreign ministry officials in June 1987, Shevardnadze indicated that the foreign policy establishment shared responsibility for the Soviet Union's decline: "If the idea that foreign policy is an extension of domestic policy is true—and it undoubtedly is true—and if the thesis that the goal of diplomacy is to form an external environment that is favorable for internal development is correct—and it undoubtedly is correct—then we are compelled to recognize that the backwardness of our power and its steady loss of status is partially our fault too."[23] He went on to criticize Soviet economic relations with the noncommunist world, describing the USSR as a "great country which in the last fifteen years has been steadily losing its position as one of the leading industrialized developed countries." He indicated that Soviet diplomats had contributed to this decline: "we frequently encouraged and at times even induced enormous material investments in foreign policy projects and tacitly promoted actions which have cost the people dearly."[24]

The interaction of domestic and foreign policy was thus designed to advance the economic dimension of Soviet security—reducing international tensions in the hope of reducing military spending, increasing investment in the civilian sector, and opening up opportunities for increased trade in the international economic system. The anticipated result was the ability to focus on "butter" rather than "guns," to convert much of the more efficient military industry to support for the civilian sector, and to bolster the economic infrastructure.

The language used by Shevardnadze in 1987, while emphasizing many of the themes of new thinking, retained numerous elements of old thinking. He still referred to the competitive nature and objectives of Soviet policy, and he still indicated that the goal was to make the Soviet political model attractive, but these were themes he would reject the following year. While Shevardnadze may have been couching his argument in a traditional framework to avoid alienating members of the hierarchy who did not share his perception that the whole system was fatally flawed, it is more likely that he was only gradually recognizing how fundamentally dysfunctional the Soviet system had become, how flawed its underlying assumptions were, and how far down the road of revison new thinking ultimately would take him.

Emphasis on Diplomacy

Another assumption of new thinking was that diplomacy and political skill—not military competition—should provide the appropriate base for a successful foreign policy. Soviet experts recognized that the military buildup and expansionism of the 1970s had fostered a Western view that the Soviet Union was a dangerous power bent on the spread of communism and pursuit of conventional and nuclear weapons superiority. The result had been chronic East-West tensions, Western military expansion and modernization, and a U.S. commitment to SDI. All presented Moscow with the need to sustain a costly arms program that it could not afford.

Having decided that military competition and foreign adventurism had been counterproductive, Shevardnadze revised the content of foreign policy to emphasize political activism and problem-solving diplomacy as a means of ensuring security. He emphasized the use of diplomacy to reduce East-West tensions; arms control to curtail the arms race; cooperation within the international community; and de-ideologization of foreign policy. These policies demanded a break with the past involving a broad range of Soviet patterns of behavior.

NEW ASSUMPTIONS

The End of East-West Rivalry

Shevardnadze was one of the first statesmen to address an emerging reality: that the era of superpower military confrontation was ending and that the new era would be one of economic competition. In an article in the foreign ministry's journal on diplomacy in 1988, he wrote: "The struggle between two opposing systems is no longer a determining tendency in the present-day era. At this stage, the ability to build up material wealth at an accelerated rate . . . and to distribute it fairly, and through joint efforts to restore and protect the resources necessary for mankind's survival acquires decisive importance."[25]

The renunciation of the underlying assumption that the Soviet Union was locked in a permanent confrontation with the West, particularly the United States—an assumption that had driven Soviet policy for seventy years—produced the radical policies of 1985–90. Arms control initiatives, unilateral force reductions, human rights concessions, withdrawal from Eastern Europe, and retreat from the Third World all derived from this basic fundamental change in perception. The Soviet Union and the

United States were no longer engaged in a life-or-death struggle from which one must emerge victorious.

De-ideologization

Shevardnadze has claimed that his skepticism about the primacy of ideology had its roots in his childhood when his relatives disagreed over political issues and he was unable to side against any of his relatives. Whatever the cause of his skepticism, throughout his career Shevardnadze adapted to his environment and pursued policies that were realistic, not dogmatic. During his years as party leader in Georgia, his approach was pragmatic not ideological, and he often felt the need to "ignore" Marxist-Leninist teachings in order to make the system function better.[26]

Shevardnadze's conviction that giving primacy to ideology over practical experience was a mistake became increasingly clear during his tenure as foreign minister, both in his actions and in his rhetoric. In an extraordinary speech to the foreign ministry in July 1988, he began his campaign to remove ideology as the basis of foreign policy, asserting that there was no longer any connection between foreign policy and the class struggle. He became the first Soviet spokesman to explicitly formalize the de-ideologization of Soviet foreign policy.[27] His article the following month, arguing that the struggle between two opposing class systems was no longer relevant to the international system, continued this effort.

It was extremely important that the leadership attack the ideological base of foreign policy decision-making. While over the years Soviet foreign policy had been largely pragmatic and aimed at advancing state interests, the underlying ideological assumptions had created the framework for thinking about the international environment. Victor Israelyan writes that, during the Arab-Israeli war of 1973, for example, "The Kremlin leaders were unanimous in favoring strict implementation of the principal Leninist foreign policy of the Soviet Union, which called for support 'of the national liberation movements and people fighting to end colonial oppression' and opposing 'the policy of the U.S. imperialist circles that is a threat to peace.' "[28] He goes on to recount the various positions taken by members of the Politburo, most of them based on traditional balance-of-power considerations, institutional biases, and realpolitik. The fact that all arguments had to be consistent with the underlying view of a world divided between socialists and imperialists, however, was a serious constraint on the radical redefinition of Soviet policy that Shevardnadze was advocating. Shevardnadze's heresy did not go unchallenged.

Yegor Ligachev, who by 1988 had become the primary conservative challenger to the new leadership's direction, considered Shevardnadze's assertions a fundamental departure from the ideological underpinnings of the system he was committed to defend. In a speech in August 1988, he defended the principle that Shevardnadze had just rejected, insisting that class struggle must remain the basis of Soviet foreign policy.[29] In this speech, delivered in Gorki, Ligachev surfaced his ideological dispute with Shevardnadze, rejecting cooperation with capitalist countries and charging that the foreign minister's abandonment of class struggle in foreign policy "introduced confusion into the thinking of Soviet people and our friends abroad."[30]

Shevardnadze abandoned Marxist-Leninist ideology before Gorbachev did. The general secretary continued to use ideological formulations, speaking of the class struggle, the dialectical approach to political thinking, and adherence to Leninist principles. In contrast, by the time of his speech to the USSR Supreme Soviet in October 1989, Shevardnadze was no longer making references to socialism or to Marxist-Leninist ideology. Rather, he stated, Soviet policy would now be guided not by Leninist norms but by "common human values." In this regard he was once again out in front of Gorbachev.

Demilitarization

Gorbachev, Shevardnadze, and Yakovlev believed that only deep cutbacks in defense spending could pay for economic reform, and they therefore favored major reductions in personnel, procurement, and research and development. Driven by a deteriorating economic situation in the Soviet Union, they believed that a critical requirement for the success of new thinking was the demilitarization of Soviet policy and society. During the Brezhnev era the military had wielded inordinate influence and power, and much of Soviet external behavior, particularly the expansionism of the 1970s, had been driven by the combination of ideology, party orthodoxy, and military thinking.

Demilitarization meant removing the military monopoly in formulating national security policy, which required dispelling assumptions about the military and challenging former policies. Shevardnadze's commentary on these subjects formed a comprehensive critique of military decision-making since the end of World War II.[31] He challenged the role of nuclear weapons, calling the bombings of Hiroshima and Nagasaki a distortion of the "identity and life" of humanity that turned postwar developments into an "atmosphere of fear and uncertainty."[32] He maintained that Soviet policy had contributed to this atmosphere, challenging the traditional Soviet line that Moscow's military buildup actually had facilitated the transition from Cold War to détente. He charged that Moscow had erred in not trying to settle fundamental political differences with the West, end the Sino-Soviet dispute, and reverse the harmful impact on détente of Soviet behavior in the Third World.

Shevardnadze became the spearhead of the new leadership's efforts to reduce the political leverage of the military and to civilianize the formulation of national security policy. Demilitarization meant creating civilian counterparts to provide both alternative counsel and serious input to national security decision-making. He sought to demilitarize Soviet society by calling in 1988 for an end both to conscription and to compulsory military classes in universities. In his speeches, he regularly attacked past military decisions and pressed for cuts in military spending. With Gorbachev's cautious (and eventually hypocritical) backing, he took the lead in demanding that the military be held accountable for the Tbilisi massacre of April 1989.[33]

Shevardnadze's critique of military policy covered every aspect of policy important to the General Staff. He called for strategic and conventional force reductions, accepted intrusive verification and asymmetry as elements of disarmament pacts, and suggested that British and French weapons be left out of the INF treaty, thus opening the door to an agreement in 1987. He attacked the military's monopoly on access to sensitive data and demanded declassification of information on the defense budget and force levels. He criticized the military's preoccupation with accumulating weaponry, noting that "security does not mean having more weapons ourselves, but having fewer weapons aimed against us."[34]

The concept of "reasonable sufficiency" introduced by the new leadership was a challenge to the military's desire for quantitative superiority, the goal that had driven defense spending to record levels in the 1970s. Shevardnadze used "reasonable sufficiency" to justify disarmament agreements for nuclear, conventional, and chemical weapons. This in turn led to bitter disputes with the defense establishment over the INF treaty in 1987, the chemical weapons ban in 1990, and the CFE treaty in 1990. The military made little attempt to hide its disdain for what it considered "self-promoting dilettantes" trying to encroach on its territory.[35]

Doctrinal changes meant that national security problems had to be resolved with the Western powers and that there could be no delay in negotiations with the United States. Sadly, U.S. policymakers failed, as late as 1989, to understand that these efforts, particularly the "civilianization of defense policy" had created the conditions for easing East-West competition and ending the Cold War.

Shevardnadze told the 19th Communist Party Conference in 1988 that Soviet diplomacy had to be shifted from a military to a political axis to deal with international issues and that, as a result, Moscow would have to limit military activities to its own territory. The following year, he told the U.N. General Assembly that Moscow's "fundamental goal is not to have a single Soviet soldier outside the country" and reported to the Supreme Soviet that the USSR was prepared to liquidate all foreign bases and pull back within its borders by the year 2000—objectives that were met five years ahead of schedule.[36]

The withdrawal from Afghanistan, announced in February 1988 and completed in March 1989, contributed to public disillusionment with the military and helped to create the groundwork for political revolution in Eastern Europe. Shevardnadze's support for total withdrawal of forces from Czechoslovakia and Hungary led to agreements in 1990 and total withdrawal in 1991, which the General Staff opposed. The Soviet navy began to withdraw unilaterally from the Mediterranean Sea, the Indian Ocean, and the South China Sea during this period.

In a speech to the 28th Party Congress in 1990, Shevardnadze referred to the fact that he had been criticized for making concessions in the sphere of security. He argued that, although strong armed forces are necessary, subordination of all else to that need is self-defeating: "Obviously . . . if we are to continue in the previous way, comrades, I declare on my own responsibility that spending one quarter of our budget on military expenditure, we will have ruined the country. We will simply have no need for defense, as we will have no need for an army for a ruined country and a poverty-stricken people."[37]

Reducing the Role of the Party

The authority of the central institutions of the Soviet Union had been in decline for many years before Gorbachev's accession to power. For this reason, Moscow did not have the option of following the Chinese example of forcing economic reform from the top and maintaining an authoritarian political structure. Soviet leaders could make decisions and implement them only when those decisions did not challenge the mid-level bureaucracy. That was the lesson Khrushchev had learned when he tried to implement reform in the 1950s, and it remained applicable in 1985.[38]

The party apparatus had become increasingly slack, undisciplined, and corrupt during Brezhnev's tenure as general secretary. At the same time, the economy had declined and the quality of life had suffered. This in turn caused Brezhnev's personal power and the party's dominance to be challenged by the KGB under Andropov. After Brezhnev's death, Andropov tried to reshape the party into an effective instrument for revitalizing the economy and society. His successor, Chernenko, a defender of the apparat's privileges and comforts, was in turn succeeded by Gorbachev, leader of the surviving Andropov coalition. The effect of these three closely contested successions was to further weaken the apparatus without reforming it.

In contrast to Andropov's attempt to reinvigorate the party apparat, Gorbachev distanced himself from it and created his own presidential councils designed to take power from the party. Until their break, Gorbachev exploited Boris Yeltsin's populist criticisms of the party to spearhead his own efforts to weaken the influence of the apparatchiks. However, Yeltsin went too far too fast for Gorbachev, publicly criticizing the stultifying influence of the party. At the 27th Party Congress in February 1986 he called for a complete reorganization of the central committee apparatus to end duplication with the economic ministries. At the subsequent plenum of the central committee, in October 1987, Yeltsin precipitated a dramatic confrontation, blaming the party for the slow pace of perestroika and specifically attacking the party secretariat, particularly Ligachev and, to a lesser extent, Gorbachev. The result was an overwhelming defense of the secretariat and of Ligachev by the rest of the leadership. Not ready to support Yeltsin, both Shevardnadze and Gorbachev strongly supported Ligachev.[39]

By permitting Ligachev to become second secretary in charge of cadres, Gorbachev had provided a potential rival with a base of resistance to his policies. The subsequent Gorbachev-Ligachev struggle culminated in the spring and summer of 1988 in the so-called "Andreyeva letter." This primitive "Stalinist" attack on perestroika and glasnost, written by a schoolteacher, was published in the provincial press while Gorbachev and Shevardnadze were in Yugoslavia. Ligachev's role in encouraging the publication was assumed, if never proved, and he praised the letter in a meeting with newspaper editors in March 1988. Gorbachev used these events to move against Ligachev, ousting him as second secretary and depriving him of his responsibilities for cadres and ideology.[40] But it was clear that the battle against reform was far from over.

The 19th Party Conference of June 1988 stripped the party secretariat of its traditional functions and removed the party from its dominant role in the political system. It also articulated a vision of Soviet democracy, creating a new Congress of People's Deputies. Measures taken at this conference spelled the effective demise of the secretariat, which rarely met thereafter.[41]

The party suffered a great defeat in the elections for the Congress of People's Deputies in March 1989, raising serious questions about its ability to continue to dominate politics in the Soviet Union. Gorbachev pressed ahead with efforts to reform the party, however, forcing large numbers of apparatchiks to resign at the April 1989 plenum. He showed little awareness that he was creating a serious political vacuum by destroying the existing mechanism before creating a viable new one to replace it. The institutional void contributed to the deterioration of the economy and the increasing nationalist ferment developing throughout the Caucasus and the Baltics during 1989 and 1990.[42]

By early 1990 the campaign to force the Communist Party to surrender its political monopoly had reached its peak. The March 1990 elections advanced Gorbachev's program of transferring policymaking authority from the party apparat to regional authorities. But the elections also revealed the weakness of his strategy. He may have hoped that by loosening the grip of the central apparatus on the country, he would strengthen his own personal authority over the party and local soviets. Yeltsin secured the needed majority in the Russian republic, however, while the party apparatus wavered between Gorbachev's candidate and one with views similar to those of Ligachev. Despite his attainment of the office of President of the Soviet Union, Gorbachev lacked a strong political base in either the party apparatus or the territorial soviets, now controlled by liberals. As a result, he was increasingly challenged in the heart of the empire, in Russia itself.

Shevardnadze had long known that reform of domestic policy required changes in foreign policy. He realized too late that the reverse was also the case: without the necessary success in domestic politics, the new foreign policy was threatened.[43] He acknowledged this point in late 1989: "Perestroika . . . predetermines the need for a fundamentally different foreign policy. But the reception given to this policy and the external response to it depend directly on the consistency and irreversibility of perestroika."[44]

Shevardnadze did not anticipate that the weakening of the political apparatus would undermine Moscow's ability to respond to the political and economic crises of 1990 and 1991. The spread of nationalist and even separatist feelings, which caused a backlash in the Russian republic, gradually overwhelmed all Soviet institutions. The military had been discredited and the party disenfranchised. Shevardnadze had played a major role in these developments, which would have the unintended and unforeseen result of precipitating the collapse of the Soviet Union itself.

Shevardnadze in Tbilisi in the early 1980s, when he was First Secretary of the Georgian Communist Party, a position he held from 1972 to 1985. During these early years in Georgia, Shevardnadze battled corruption and introduced the most liberal political and economic reforms of any Soviet regional leader.

Unless otherwise indicated, all pictures are courtesy of the Government of Georgia.

Shevardnadze giving a speech during his days as party leader in Georgia. When Gorbachev appointed him Soviet foreign minister in 1985, he became the first Soviet spokesman to formalize explicitly the de-ideologization of Soviet foreign policy.

Shevardnadze with General Secretary Mikhail Gorbachev and U.S. President Ronald Reagan at the Reykjavik summit in 1986. At the far right is U.S. Secretary of State George P. Shultz. Shultz and Shevardnadze agree that Reykjavik helped convince a skeptical Reagan that the Kremlin was serious about arms control.

On a plane with longtime aide and speechwriter Teimuraz Mamaladze-Stepanov in 1992. Stepanov accompanied Shevardnadze to Moscow in 1985 and returned with him to Tbilisi in 1992. Having spent seven years in Moscow, Shevardnadze returned to rebuild a Georgia torn by internal strife and international isolation.

Shevardnadze with Secretary of State James Baker in Tbilisi in May 1992. Despite the difficult security situation in Tbilisi, and against the advice of his aides, Baker flew to Georgia immediately after the conference on the Middle East in Madrid, to demonstrate his support for the former Soviet foreign minister.

Shevardnadze meets with German Foreign Minister Hans-Dietrich Genscher in Tbilisi in April 1992. Among foreign ministers in the West, Genscher was the first to recognize the importance of Shevardnadze's "new political thinking" and to encourage a strategic dialogue with the Soviet foreign minister.

At the United Nations with Secretary General Boutros Boutros-Ghali in 1992, after discussing peacekeeping issues in Abkhazia and South Ossetia.

Shevardnadze welcomes Turkish Prime Minister Sulaymin Demirel to Tbilisi in July 1992, to discuss Turkish investment in Caspian oil pipelines through Georgia. Oil is critical for Georgia's economic future, and in 1996 Turkey agreed to spend $350 million to overhaul Georgian pipelines.

Abkhazia's bid for independence was just one crisis facing Shevardnadze at home. Here he is shown in Helsinki in 1992, where he was trying to get the Conference on Security and Cooperation in Europe to make a commitment to peacekeeping in Abkhazia in order to avoid Georgian reliance on Russian forces.

Shevardnadze with guards in the Abkhaz capital of Sukhumi in the summer of 1993, during some of the worst fighting. According to Shevardnadze, "I was searching for death from shells and missiles in the streets."

Surveying the devastated city of Sukhumi in September 1993. Claiming he would stay until the end, Shevardnadze finally was forced to flee the city hours before Russian-backed Abkhaz separatists captured it.

Shevardnadze meets with Russian President Boris Yeltsin during a visit to Moscow in October 1993. In return for Moscow's military assistance in Abkhazia, Shevardnadze accepted a greater Russian presence in Georgia. Although the rebellion was soon suppressed, many Georgians resented Shevardnadze's deal with the Russians.

Enjoying a rare light moment during a flight to Washington for a state visit in March 1994. Feeling as though he had few international allies, Shevardnadze had low expectations for securing U.S. aid and support.

Shevardnadze with President Bill Clinton during a state visit to the United States in March 1994. *Top*: Clinton welcomes Shevardnadze to the White House. *Bottom*: Both men field questions during a press conference. No state dinner was held for the Georgian president, and the visit yielded only $70 million in assistance for Georgia.

During Shevardnadze's state visit in March 1994, U.S. Secretary of State James Baker arranged a dinner party at Blair House with U.S. businessmen to encourage private investment in Georgia, but with no success. To Shevardnadze's left are then Foreign Minister Alexander Chikvaidze and longtime aide Teimuraz Mamaladze-Stepanov.

In deep thought at the Georgian parliament. The years since his return to Georgia have been lonely ones for Shevardnadze. (*ITAR-TASS/SOVFOTO*)

Former Secretary of State George P. Shultz with Shevardnadze in 1994. Shultz had liked Shevardnadze from the start, finding him a welcome relief from the dour Andrey Gromyko.

With Zbigniew Brzezinski, U.S. national security adviser under President Jimmy Carter, on a visit to Tbilisi in December 1994. Brzezinski and Shevardnadze discussed many international issues, particularly those related to the Caucasus and the Balkans.

Shevardnadze receives congratulations from Georgia's Patriarch Ilia II after inauguration as Georgia's president in November 1995. The inauguration took place in the ancient cathedral in Mtskheta.

Shevardnadze in Tbilisi with Georgians in their "chokhas," traditional dress in the Caucasus.

In the streets of Tbilisi. Shevardnadze has become more popular with the people as the Georgian economy has made headway in reversing its economic freefall after the dissolution of the Soviet Union.

Answering questions in Georgia. Shevardnadze could have retired from public life in 1991 as an honored statesman, but he chose instead to engage in yet another battle, this time to keep his country from self-destruction and create a viable government.

Meeting with U.S. Ambassador to the United Nations Madeleine Albright in Tbilisi in 1995. One of Shevardnadze's continuing battles is to carve out a place for Georgia in the international community.

Shevardnadze prepares to address the Georgian parliament in 1995. A brilliant and ruthless political infighter, he relishes the challenge of bringing stability to his newly independent state.

4

ROCKING THE BOAT

Shevardnadze Battles the Bureaucracy

The fact that the foreign policy service—one of the most important and most sensitive links in the system of state management— pursued obligations out of touch with the country's fundamental vital interests is on our conscience.
—Eduard Shevardnadze

To pursue their foreign policy goals successfully, Gorbachev and Shevardnadze had to take on entrenched bureaucracies accustomed to pursuing long-established agendas. They had to persuade, co-opt, or force these institutions and the officials who ran them to accept new assumptions and directions. They were enormously successful during the five years of their partnership, implementing profound changes in their country and its institutions and policies, and taking the Soviet Union into a revolution directed from the top. In weakening the institutions that enforced the status quo, however, Gorbachev and Shevardnadze failed to build new institutions that might have enabled them to prevail over the opponents of perestroika and delay the collapse of the Soviet Union. Ambassador Anatoly Dobrynin accused Gorbachev of having become a "virtual monarch, bypassing the traditional policymaking institutions."[1]

Shevardnadze's first challenge, the foreign ministry, was under his direct control, and within a year of becoming foreign minister he had turned Andrey Gromyko's moribund institution into the major player in the foreign policy establishment. He accomplished this by rejuvenating the ministry, enhancing the role of diplomacy in national security policy, and usurping the functions of competing institutions in the party apparatus. Despite Shevardnadze's successful co-option of the ministry, officials (such as First Deputy Foreign Minister Korniyenko, Ambassador Dobrynin, and leading Arabist Yevgeny Primakov) maintained their opposition to many of his policies. In the last year of his tenure they participated in undermining his policies and position.

Challenging the military's leading role in defining national security policy was perhaps the single most important aspect of the Gorbachev-Shevardnadze approach to reform. Reducing the military budget was crucial to perestroika; easing tensions in the international environment and improving relations with the United States were central to new thinking. Since Gorbachev did not appoint a proponent of radical reform to head the defense ministry, Shevardnadze became the point man in the effort to weaken the military establishment. He and Gorbachev were extremely successful in pushing through radical arms control proposals, implementing unilateral force reductions, overseeing the withdrawal from Eastern Europe, and accomplishing the retreat from the Third World. In the end, however, their military antagonists joined with other opponents to defeat Shevardnadze and weaken Gorbachev.

Finally, in order to gain control over the formulation and implementation of foreign policy, Shevardnadze had to preempt the Communist Party institutions involved in national security policy: the Politburo and the foreign ministry's main bureaucratic rival, the Central Committee's International Department. Gorbachev transferred some functions to new presidential commissions, and Shevardnadze's assertive advancement of his policies enabled him to render the international department virtually irrelevant to the policy process. Conservative party leaders, such as Ligachev, remained active and critical, however, and eventually helped to precipitate the fall of Shevardnadze and Gorbachev.

Shevardnadze had creative ideas for institutionalizing policy—a rare attribute among leaders in any society—but as foreign minister he was limited in his ability to impose these ideas outside of the foreign ministry. A fatal flaw in the approach he and Gorbachev took was to weaken the existing institutions of power without replacing them. They challenged the traditional powers of the central committee, the defense council, the

General Staff, and the KGB. But there were no legitimate institutions to pick up those powers, and the institutions themselves remained staffed with opponents, many of whom would participate in the failed coup against Gorbachev in 1991.

Gorbachev and Shevardnadze did not create effective policymaking institutions because of their authoritarian style, a legacy of their Soviet past. Increasingly, they relied on their own views and less on consultation with others. This tendency, which intensified after the signing of the INF treaty at the Washington summit in 1987, antagonized conservatives who had wielded authority in the past and distrusted the direction new thinking was taking. It also alienated liberals who believed that reform should include more democratization.

REBUILDING THE FOREIGN MINISTRY

Uprooting Gromyko's Legacy

Shevardnadze was unlike his predecessors in many respects. He was not Russian, and he lacked the typical Russian distrust of the West; he was a Georgian, given to innovative thinking and bold actions. He was not a diplomat, cautious and immersed in the complexities of international discourse; he was a politician, committed to solving problems and impatient with obstacles. Previous foreign ministers had been subservient to the party; he was a close colleague of Gorbachev's and believed he had the Soviet leader's imprimatur to effect change.[2]

Shevardnadze was very unlike Gromyko in disposition and approach. He had no patience with the confrontational style of his predecessor, and he brought to the ministry a penchant for pragmatism and active problem-solving. The dour and obedient Gromyko, who according to Khrushchev would have "pulled down his pants and sat on a block of ice" if told to do so, rarely showed any emotion and suffered from the sense of personal insecurity fostered by the Stalinist system. Former Secretary of State Henry Kissinger observed that Gromyko seemed to be "seized by an undefinable terror that his opposite number might pull some last-minute trick on him."[3] Whereas Gromyko cautiously waited for instructions, Shevardnadze took the lead in creating and implementing policy.

Shevardnadze knew that policy had become stale and unproductive under Gromyko. He criticized the ministry for failing to "deliver the warning signals about our lagging behind in the scientific-technical revolution," to predict structural changes in the world economy, and "to caution against lopsided infatuation with trade in energy products."[4] At the 27th Party Congress in February 1986, he accused Gromyko of creating obstacles to diplomacy and warned against the "senseless stubbornness" that had earned Soviet ministers the label "Mr. Nyet," particularly in Washington.[5]

Anticipating resistance to new thinking, Shevardnadze arranged for Gorbachev to endorse change at an unusual foreign ministry conference in early 1986.[6] The president told the assembled diplomats that it was time to end the lethargy of the Gromyko era and introduce new thinking to the conduct of foreign policy. Not all members of the foreign ministry took Gorbachev's message to heart. Dobrynin and Korniyenko actually increased their criticism of Shevardnadze, arguing that policy reform was difficult and that "fierce clashes, sharp discussions, and painful differences are inevitable." Nonetheless, armed with the president's mandate, Shevardnadze was ready to move.

The Key: Changing Personnel

Shevardnadze recognized that much of the old foreign ministry guard would have to go. In his first three years, he replaced a large percentage of the ministry's top officers, including the two first deputy ministers, seven deputies, and ambassadors to most important countries. His action was not a simple changing of the guard; it involved the promotion of younger, better-educated officials with expertise in their fields. With the exception of Teimuraz Mamaladze-Stepanov, his senior aide for two decades, he did not bring in members of his Georgian retinue.

Shevardnadze changed the demographics of the foreign ministry in several years. By 1989 nearly 80 percent of the diplomatic service were under the age of fifty, and only three percent were over sixty. He promoted younger officers and recruited more women and non-Russians, introducing more than one hundred women and "representatives of forty nations and nationalities" to key diplomatic posts.[7] In view of the size of the foreign ministry—nearly 4,000 personnel in Moscow and nearly 10,000 abroad—the number of women and minorities was still small. He strengthened the role of the diplomatic academy and placed far more emphasis on training than Gromyko had.[8] He did this with a relatively small budget, never more than $2 billion a year.

Out with "Nyet," in with the New

In his most decisive move, Shevardnadze removed First Deputy Foreign Ministers Korniyenko and Viktor Maltsev. Maltsev, an engineer and Brezhnev protégé, had been rewarded with diplomatic assignments for which he was unqualified. Korniyenko, on the other hand, was an outstanding diplomat and a logical successor to Gromyko. Gorbachev considered him the ministry's leading expert on arms control and used him accordingly until Korniyenko, known for his anti-U.S. views and opposition to perestroika, wore out his welcome with both Shevardnadze and Secretary of State Shultz. When Shevardnadze pushed him aside in 1986, he moved over to the Central Committee's International Department, where he served as deputy to Anatoly Dobrynin.

Dobrynin, also a contender for Shevardnadze's job, was named chief of the International Department when he returned from his long tour as ambassador in Washington in 1986. He and the department became increasingly irrelevant to the policy process. Both Dobrynin and Korniyenko retired in 1989, but they continued to write essays criticizing Shevardnadze and his policies. Dobrynin refused to be interviewed for this book, claiming that Shevardnadze "was a good friend of mine, but I have nothing good to say about him."[9]

The new first deputy foreign ministers, Yuly Vorontsov and Anatoly Kovalev, were outstanding diplomats with extensive experience in East-West relations. Vorontsov had been posted in Afghanistan, France, India, and the United States, where he had been minister-counselor of the embassy for ten years; in 1994, he would become the Russian ambassador to the United States. Kovalev, a deputy foreign minister for fifteen years, was a proponent of unilateral troop reductions in Europe and a critic of long-standing Soviet efforts to drive a wedge between the United States and Western Europe.[10]

Shevardnadze replaced most deputy ministers, including Leonid Ilichev and the late Mikhail Kapitsa, who represented a generation of Stalinist diplomats. Ilichev, a specialist on ideology under Khrushchev, was a respected philosopher and a gentleman. Shevardnadze saw no risk in keeping him around and did not fire him immediately.[11] Eventually, however, he was replaced by Igor Rogachev, a leading Sinologist and serious scholar. Kapitsa had a serious drinking problem and was a womanizer, according to Ambassador Israelyan; on one occasion, he was physically attacked by his driver, with whose wife he was having an affair. Shevardnadze fired Kapitsa after the latter became so drunk during the foreign minister's first trip to Asia in 1986 that he could not even attend important ministerial meetings in Ulan Bator; the following year he became director of the Institute of Asia.[12]

Shevardnadze promoted many officials whose background was in U.S. and European affairs, reflecting his focus on improved relations with the West. Bessmertnykh, a former chief of the USA section, became deputy minister with responsibility for policy toward Washington in 1986. Bessmertnykh had become a major adviser to Shevardnadze early in the foreign minister's tenure. Before the first meeting between Shevardnadze and Shultz in September 1985, Bessmertnykh informed Shevardnadze that the top item on the agenda would be strategic arms. For two weeks, Shevardnadze and Bessmertnykh met nearly every day to review the numbers, ranges, and types of nuclear weapons—subjects that seemed like "higher mathematics" to Shevardnadze.[13] He relied heavily on Bessmertnykh during this period and praised him as the foreign ministry's chief troubleshooter. Bessmertnykh would become ambassador to the United States in 1990 and would succeed Shevardnadze as foreign minister in 1991. Two other new deputy foreign ministers, Vladimir Petrovsky and Anatoly Adamishin, were European specialists who, under Shevardnadze, would monitor Third World issues for their impact on East-West relations.

Shevardnadze promoted a number of specialists who had criticized Soviet policy in the past. His special assistant for the Middle East, Gennady Tarasov, had developed good ties with Israeli counterparts at the United Nations and had criticized Moscow's close ties to radical Arab states. The new deputy chief for African affairs, Boris Asoyan, had written a devastating critique of Brezhnev's African policy. The department chief for Southeast Asia, Vladimir Lukin, who would become ambassador to the United States in 1992, had been critical of Soviet policy toward China.

As head of the Near East Department, Shevardnadze named Vladimir Polyakov, an expert on Arab-Israeli affairs for more than twenty-five years, who had argued for a more flexible policy.[14] Like other influential regional specialists under Shevardnadze, Polyakov had served at the embassy in Washington.[15] In view of the lack of Third World expertise on the part of Shevardnadze and his key deputies—Kovalev, Bessmert-nykh, and Vorontsov—Polyakov occupied an unusually influential position. In 1988, he became the first Soviet official to visit Saudi Arabia in more than fifty years.

Nevertheless, Shevardnadze made the mistake of leaving in place several high-level officials of the old school: Valentin Falin, Viktor Komplektov, and Yuly Kvitsinsky, who might well have become foreign minister in 1991 if the coup against Gorbachev had been successful.[16] Kvitsinsky and Falin opposed Shevardnadze's position on German reunification, and Komplektov resisted close ties with the United States.

New Emissaries

Shevardnadze's new ambassadors were far more moderate and, on average, fifteen years younger than their predecessors, but some of the appointments were questionable. Yury Dubinin was named ambassador to Washington in 1986, only two months after he had been named ambassador to the United Nations, suggesting confusion and possible infighting. He had close ties to Kovalev, but he had serious substantive and linguistic limitations.[17] Dubinin never became a player in Washington and, according to Shultz, was "not a real heavyweight."[18] Kvitsinsky became ambassador to Bonn and then deputy minister in 1989, a move designed to enhance his role in talks on unification. He became the sole deputy for Europe, where previously there had been two—one for the East and another for the West—but his anti-German views tended to slow the pace of negotiations rather than facilitate them.

Shevardnadze wanted to change the credentials of diplomats going to Eastern Europe, no longer posting party officials who resisted reform but appointing diplomats with regional expertise. The new ambassadors to Eastern Europe—particularly Ivan Aboimov (Hungary), Yury Kashlev (Poland), and Boris Pankin (Czechoslovakia)—were regional experts. Pankin replaced Bessmertnykh as foreign minister for a brief period in 1991, following the aborted coup attempt in August, because he was one of the few ambassadors who refused to follow the orders of the coup leaders.[19]

In his last year as foreign minister, Shevardnadze again tried to inject new life into his policies by assigning new ambassadors to key posts: Bonn, Paris, Rome, Washington, all the former Warsaw Pact member states, and the United Nations. *Izvestia* explained that it was necessary

to fill these posts with "competent people who think along modern
lines." In Eastern Europe, where the Soviets were negotiating troop
withdrawals and acquiescing in the demise of the Warsaw Pact, Shevardnadze wanted diplomats of "another type and character."[20] His new
appointees were careerists or intellectuals: a writer and journalist for
Prague and an ambassador fluent in Romanian and Hungarian for Bucha-
rest, where the problem of the Hungarian minority was a major issue.

Reorganization

In addition to changing personnel, Shevardnadze reorganized the foreign
ministry for the first time since the end of World War II. He reduced the
number of regional departments from eighteen to twelve and created a
number of functional departments. In creating the arms control and
disarmament administration and the peaceful uses of atomic energy and
space department, he signaled that issues of arms control would no longer
be left to the military. Viktor Karpov, former chief of the START
delegation, became head of the arms control group. Vladimir Shustov, a
veteran arms control negotiator, became head of a new scientific coordination center designed to expand contacts between the foreign ministry
and the academy of sciences on disarmament issues.[21]

A human rights and cultural ties administration was established in
1986 to monitor human rights, an issue important to the new foreign
minister because of its importance to the United States. Focusing on
human rights came easily to Shevardnadze, who had been an early
supporter of emigration of Jews to Israel. Even when Soviet rates of
emigration slowed to a trickle in the 1970s, Georgian Jews were able to
find a way out. He continued this policy in 1992 on his return to Tbilisi,
where his efforts on behalf of Jews and other minorities angered Georgia's
ultranationalists.[22]

Shevardnadze merged the ministry's information department and press
department into a new information administration. He recruited Gennady Gerasimov, the editor of the *Moscow News*, to create the new
department, hoping to avoid the public relations problems that accompanied Gorbachev's first summit meeting with President Ronald Reagan in
1985 and the Chernobyl tragedy of 1986, when the ministry denied that
a disaster had occurred.[23] Traditionalists in the foreign ministry initially
denied Gerasimov the rank and salary of ambassador and referred dispar-

agingly to his department as a section (*otdel*). Thanks to Shevardnadze, Gerasimov eventually received his higher rank and salary. Shevardnadze insisted that Gerasimov receive all embassy cables so that he could respond quickly and authoritatively in press conferences. During Shevardnadze's trips abroad, Gerasimov had far more latitude to respond to questions than his predecessors had.

Shevardnadze also made changes in the ministry's regional departments. Recognizing the importance of Europe and the centrality of disarmament, he created a new Institute of Europe in 1987, headed by Vitaly Zhurkin, an arms control expert and former deputy director of the Institute of the USA and Canada. Shevardnadze consolidated Eastern European affairs into a single department and placed a deputy minister in charge of the region. This demonstrated his intention to put relations with Eastern Europe on a state-to-state rather than party-to-party basis.[24] During the Gromyko era, the foreign ministry had deferred to the Central Committee in orchestrating policy in the region.

Glasnost

Arguing that lack of openness was one of the causes of serious foreign policy blunders, such as Afghanistan, Shevardnadze proposed to openly confront the mistakes of the past, calling for glasnost in foreign as well as domestic policy.[25] He stated that such unwise decisions as the invasion of Afghanistan, the deployment of SS-20 medium-range missiles, and construction of the Krasnoyarsk radar in violation of the ABM treaty would not have been made if they had been openly debated.

Before Shevardnadze and new thinking, it was not possible to find references to mistakes or blunders in Soviet writing on foreign policy. Shevardnadze himself, before 1988, rued the fact that, under glasnost, controversial articles could be found on internal affairs, particularly economic and cultural issues, but there had been nothing similar in foreign policy. "Can it really be," Shevardnadze asked, "that we have everything right and there are no other options than the ones that are being followed now?"[26] Shevardnadze extended glasnost to foreign affairs and started a process that produced far-reaching change in security policy.

The bureaucracy was slow to respond to calls for openness, however. No officials criticized mistakes, particularly the Afghan offensives in 1985 and 1986 and the sham withdrawal in 1986. Shevardnadze knew that the press handling of Chernobyl was a public relations disaster, but even his own commentary contained skewed accounts of the tragedy.[27] Of course, Shevardnadze himself had never been known for criticizing his patrons.

Shevardnadze called on foreign ministry officials to report accurately, and he criticized embassies for tailoring the "facts of life to established notions" of the Kremlin or trying to "please the center with an embellished picture of events."[28] He upgraded the quality of the information and intelligence on which foreign policy was based, making sure that experts in the foreign ministry worked more closely with their counterparts in the research centers of Moscow's institutes of science. Shevardnadze distrusted the KGB and developed his own intelligence network, using experts in the foreign ministry and the academic world to analyze international developments.[29] Shevardnadze ordered the declassification of data and introduced a new bimonthly on foreign policy, *Bulletin of the Foreign Ministry of the USSR*, which published official documents and became an outlet for civilian critics of the military.[30]

Using Think Tanks

Shevardnadze told a ministry conference in 1988 that it was essential to solicit the views of outside experts and to recruit younger analysts. He encouraged these analysts to challenge conventional wisdom on national security issues and used their work to justify sensitive political decisions. Their efforts supported the nuclear test moratorium that was declared in 1985 and the unilateral troop cut in 1988, both heavily criticized by the military.

The role of foreign affairs institutes also expanded during Shevardnadze's tenure. The foreign minister named institute officials to important positions at the foreign ministry and as advisers to arms control delegations. The Institute of World Economics and International Relations (IMEMO) became the preeminent think tank during Shevardnadze's tenure. The new director of IMEMO, Yevgeny Primakov, initially supported Shevardnadze's foreign and security policy in the 1980s and gradually became more prominent than his major rival Georgy Arbatov, the longtime head of the Institute of the United States and Canada. In 1989, Primakov moved from IMEMO to the Politburo, where he opposed many of Shevardnadze's policies.

Aleksey Arbatov, chief of IMEMO's arms control department and son of the director of the USA Institute, was one of the foreign minister's advisers on arms control and security issues. Like Shevardnadze, he believed that the concept of "victory" was meaningless in the nuclear age because of the destructive power of strategic weaponry. He favored drastic cuts in strategic warheads and contributed to the debate on "reasonable sufficiency."[31] Arbatov charged that military secrecy inhibited the ability of disarmament experts to provide useful analyses for policymakers, especially in calculating cuts needed to meet the requirements of "reasonable sufficiency."[32] Arbatov credited Shevardnadze with encouraging radical changes on security issues and establishing the department for disarmament in the foreign ministry, thus weakening the influence of the military on security policy.[33]

Arbatov and such colleagues as Andrey Kortunov and Sergey Karaganov challenged conventional wisdom on the nature of the U.S. threat and presented their views in authoritative journals, including the party's theoretical journal *Kommunist*. In 1988, Karaganov, Kortunov, and Vitaly Zhurkin, arguing that the USSR faced no threat of aggression from the West, asserted that the military should be restructured to reflect a more defensive character. Their articles urged the defense industries to support Gorbachev's industrial modernization programs.

Limits of Change

Shevardnadze's changes in the foreign ministry enabled the new leadership to proceed rapidly with new thinking and develop a counterweight to the military community. The strengthened ministry played a leading role in extricating the Soviet Union from Afghanistan and in facilitating its retreat from the Third World. For the first time, civilians became actively involved in the operational aspects of arms control and provided new instructions to Soviet delegations at disarmament talks.

Gorbachev and Shevardnadze widely consulted the decision-making community in their first two years in power, but in the wake of the INF treaty and the consolidation of relations with the United States such consultation virtually ceased. Shevardnadze's personal diplomacy with Shultz and Baker solidified his position, and as a result he consulted only with Gorbachev. The president himself was aristocratic, even arrogant, in nature and not one to consult or coordinate. By 1988, therefore, the decision-making network for foreign policy consisted of Gorbachev and

Shevardnadze, and Shevardnadze's call for "democratization" of foreign policy was viewed as a sham. Foreign ministry critics joined a growing list of opponents to his authoritarian style.

The limits of change within the ministry were in evidence during the coup attempt in August 1991, when many high-ranking officials failed to support Gorbachev. Without Shevardnadze at the helm, the ministry showed political and bureaucratic cowardice. Former Foreign Minister Shevardnadze joined Yeltsin in "the White House" despite their political differences, but his successor, Bessmertnykh, called in sick. First Deputy Kvitsinsky was in charge during Bessmertnykh's diplomatic illness, and he bowed to the "Committee of Eight," sending telegrams to all embassies with instructions to inform host governments of the "change" in government in Moscow. Bessmertnykh, who was at the foreign ministry when the telegrams were sent, audaciously went to the Moscow airport to meet Gorbachev's plane after the failure of the coup. Several ambassadors courageously ignored the instructions, but most did not. Many who carried out the instructions, including ambassadors in Great Britain, Greece, and Sweden, were called back to Moscow and fired. Ambassador to Czechoslovakia Boris Pankin ignored the instructions and was promoted to foreign minister. He proved an extremely unpopular choice, however, and lacked the stature and poise for his new position, in which he lasted less than three months. Shevardnadze replaced Pankin only a month before the collapse of the Soviet Union.

TAKING ON THE MILITARY

Shevardnadze was disdainful of those who had allowed the Soviet Union to be "drawn into an arms race" with the United States, responding "symmetrically and massively, whereas we needed to respond asymmetrically at a lower quantitative but a higher qualitative level."[34] He argued that "those who have put the emphasis on military means are themselves at a disadvantage"—meaning the Politburo, the defense council, and the defense ministry.[35] Because of his close ties to Gorbachev, Shevardnadze had no fear of his opponents in these institutions.

Gorbachev and Shevardnadze were the first Soviet leaders to challenge the power of the military, and the two men worked together to demilitarize Soviet society. In order to effect deep cuts in military spending, they had to weaken the leverage of military institutions and reduce the myth of the military's infallibility. Repeated presidential calls for reduced military spending were complemented by Shevardnadze's criticism of military decisions. Previously pro forma praise for the military was conspicuously absent from their speeches. Gorbachev neither displayed nor awarded himself military decorations, and Shevardnadze never attended a military ceremony until the anniversary of the Soviet air forces in February 1990, when he was in deep political trouble. Gorbachev reduced the number of uniformed men standing on Lenin's mausoleum during official functions and banned modern weapons from the celebration of the October Revolution.

More than any other Soviet official, Shevardnadze challenged the influence and prestige of the military, becoming Gorbachev's "point man" in the struggle to reduce defense spending and deployments and to restructure decision-making on national security issues. He did so quietly, behind the scenes, during his first two years as foreign minister, but with the success of the INF treaty he openly took on the military establishment. He had considerable success, pushing through a series of arms control and arms reduction measures right up until November 1990, a month before his resignation.

Confronting the Establishment

Purging the Defense Ministry

On May 28, 1987, the anniversary of the creation of border guards in the Soviet Union, a West German teenager, Mathias Rust, landed a Cessna aircraft near the gates of the Kremlin. Two days later, Gorbachev and Shevardnadze moved against the defense ministry. Their purge included the defense minister, the chief of the General Staff, the first deputy ministers, and ten of sixteen deputy ministers. Their objective was to weaken the prestige and authority of the ministry and to strengthen that of Shevardnadze and the foreign ministry.[36]

The appointment of new chiefs to the military services introduced a new era in the defense ministry, dimming its luster by removing leaders of stature who had been responsible for building the modern Soviet military. Army General Yury Maksimov replaced Marshal Vladimir Tolubko, who had built the Strategic Rocket Forces (SRF), thus diminishing the SRF. Admiral V. Chernavin became chief of the Soviet navy, replacing Admiral Sergey Gorshkov, who had transformed the navy into a modern force with global reach. Gorshkov was sent into retirement without praise.

The new defense minister, General Dmitry Yazov, a relatively junior general officer with a background in personnel, was considered a lightweight. Yazov, according to Ambassador Dobrynin, made Shevardnadze's job much easier because he knew "little" about disarmament talks and was far more obedient to Gorbachev than his predecessor, Marshal Sergey Sokolov, an old-style officer opposed to détente.[37] General Sergey Akhromeyev became chief of the General Staff, replacing Marshal Nikolay Ogarkov. One of the most brilliant officers in the Red Army, Ogarkov predicted U.S. success with high-technology weapons long before the Persian Gulf war and advocated increased spending on sophisticated weaponry to enable the Soviets to catch up. Shevardnadze wanted him removed from the chain of command, fearing he would push for an increased defense budget. Ogarkov's death in 1994 was barely observed by the government and the media, signifying how far the Russian military's prestige had fallen.[38]

The promotions of Yazov and Akhromeyev seemed to prepare the way for new thinking and perestroika in the defense ministry, with more than one hundred generals and colonels following Sokolov into retirement. Yazov's claim that modern weapons had become so destructive they could no longer be utilized, and Akhromeyev's assertion that the military's major task was to prevent war, heralded change.[39] Akhromeyev supported cuts in strategic arms and was a major player at the Reykjavik summit in 1986; U.S. officials, particularly Shultz and Baker, held him in high regard, as did Gorbachev.[40]

Shevardnadze did not share this high opinion of Akhromeyev, nor was he confident that Akhromeyev and Yazov would create a military consensus for comprehensive disarmament and radical reductions in the Soviet military. Shevardnadze was right; neither Yazov nor Akhromeyev was prepared to play a strong role in moving the military in a new direction. In the end, Akhromeyev opposed unilateral cuts in conventional arms, announcing his retirement in December 1988 on the day Gorbachev dramatically unveiled unilateral troop withdrawals at the United Nations.

The resignation of Akhromeyev as chief of the General Staff only exacerbated Shevardnadze's problems, however. Akhromeyev's successor, Mikhail Moiseyev, resented Shevardnadze's efforts to play a leading role in disarmament and argued that the foreign minister should consult with the general staff before negotiating with the United States. He was extremely critical of glasnost and contributed to a contentious debate on issues such as CFE, unilateral cutbacks, and increased autonomy for the non-Russian republics. The reemergence of other hardline elements bolstered Moiseyev's intransigence.

The failure of Gorbachev's economic policies at home and Shevardnadze's foreign policies in Eastern Europe weakened the influence of both men by the end of 1989. Soviet society and politics became increasingly chaotic, feeding the mood of separatism that was sweeping the Baltics.[41] Even military officers who supported perestroika, many of whom were elected to the Congress of People's Deputies in 1989–90, opposed Shevardnadze's policies on national security.[42]

Gorbachev and Shevardnadze succeeded in diminishing the prestige of the defense ministry, but they were not able to install a military leadership that was actively supportive of their radical agenda. They therefore had to find ways to advance their agenda without the strong backing of the military establishment. They accomplished this by broadening the base of decision-making on national security and taking preemptive action on disarmament, thus keeping the military on the defensive. In doing so, they further undermined the stature of the Soviet Union's proudest and most prestigious institution.

Broadening the Base of Decision-making

Gorbachev's first move was to place Shevardnadze and Alexander Yakovlev within the party's most important decision-making bodies on national security. Participation in sessions of the Defense Council, the most senior decision-making body since the 1920s, enabled them to review and define all decisions on force deployment, as well as all deliberations involving military strategy and doctrine. Participation in the Arms Control Coordinating Commission, established in 1988 to coordinate negotiating positions in arms control talks, allowed them to advance innovative disarmament proposals.

Shevardnadze used criticism of military decisions, such as construction of the controversial Krasnoyarsk radar site in violation of the ABM treaty, as ammunition in his drive to sponsor civilian competition with the military on strategic issues. He told a security conference in 1988 that "major innovations in defense development should be verified at the foreign ministry to determine whether they correspond juridically to existing international agreements and to stated political positions."[43] He even went so far as to demand a veto over programs presented to the Defense Council by the defense ministry.

Turning to his advisers for assistance, Shevardnadze encouraged them to debate the military on security issues dominated by the General Staff. He created special departments in the foreign ministry on national security and used their analyses to justify unilateral cuts in conventional arms as well as deep strategic reductions. The promotions of Bessmertnykh and Petrovsky, both of whom had extensive arms control experience, demonstrated that Shevardnadze planned to formulate disarmament policy within the foreign ministry.

Shevardnadze won many skirmishes in the bureaucratic tug-of-war over national security policy. The greater role for civilians in arms control and in discussions of military doctrine strengthened the influence of the foreign ministry and weakened the military. The defense ministry and the General Staff gradually lost their monopoly on the formulation of national security policy. Shevardnadze acknowledged "sharp disputes" between military and civilian experts.[44] "There were quite a few people who accused diplomats of making concessions and giving ground and not taking military interests into account," he stated in 1989.[45]

Going Around the Military

Shevardnadze became an expert at manipulating the system, using his access to Gorbachev as leverage to accomplish his objectives, according to Tarasenko.[46] After consulting with Gorbachev, he would tell the military that a position had already been approved and gain its acceptance. The attitude of military officials actually reinforced his efforts. They did not believe real change would occur, so they often agreed to initiatives they assumed would never be implemented. They were so accustomed to talks that went nowhere that they entered negotiations assuming they would fail. When negotiations conducted by Shevardnadze actually succeeded, it was too late for them to change position. The military missed so many tactical shifts in policy that it was not prepared for the radical strategic changes that occurred.

Shevardnadze's access to Gorbachev as well as his close relations with U.S. leaders gave him unique access to sensitive information, and he became the institutional memory for Soviet-American relations. The military was on the outside and had difficulty learning details of sensitive negotiations. The new imbalance between the foreign and defense ministries marked a reversal of traditional policymaking, leaving senior military officers scrambling for sensitive information on disarmament negotiations and force deployments.

Toward the end of his tenure and under attack for many of his decisions, Shevardnadze denied accusations that policies such as unilateral arms reductions had not been vetted with the military. Responding to a charge by a Soviet general that he had taken an initiative "not worked on by the Ministry of Defense,"[47] he remarked that his announcement of the unilateral withdrawal of tactical missiles from Central Europe was made "on the basis of a document signed by the defense minister and the chief of the General Staff, and presumably vetted through the Defense Council on behalf of the Politburo."[48] Military leaders, perhaps not wanting to reveal their own irrelevance to the policy process, tended to confirm Shevardnadze's claims. Moiseyev acknowledged that he had "supported Gorbachev's initiatives," and Yazov and Lev Zaykov (the senior party secretary for defense affairs) defended Gorbachev's actions with respect to arms reductions.[49]

Glasnost as Weapon

Shevardnadze carried his call for glasnost into the area of security policy, insisting on broad publication of defense data and initiating debate between civilian and military analysts on disarmament and force procurement. At a foreign ministry conference in 1988, he argued that "one of the most unfavorable phenomena of the period of stagnation that hurt our international positions was the lack of coordination between the military and policy areas."[50] The only remedy, according to Shevardnadze, was more-extensive sharing of information and greater interdepartmental cooperation in national security.

Shevardnadze encouraged journalists and researchers to challenge military viewpoints. In 1987 journalist Alexander Bovin indicated that deployment of the SS-20 in the 1970s had been counterproductive because it had led to the U.S. decision to place Pershing-2 missiles in Germany. In 1989, Deputy Foreign Minister Bessmertnykh openly attacked the Defense Council for its approval of SS-20 deployments, the first time a non-Politburo member had publicly criticized the most important decision-making institution for national security.[51]

With Shevardnadze's encouragement, Petrovsky, an arms control expert, abandoned the pseudonym he had previously used and became an open advocate of arms control and of Shevardnadze's views on foreign policy, particularly the view that the USSR "would prefer its troops not be situated anywhere outside its national borders."[52] In 1987, Petrovsky told a U.N. conference on disarmament that the published Soviet defense budget did not include weapons research and development but merely "reflected what the USSR . . . spent on personnel, logistics, military construction, and pension funds,"[53] thus confirming what some Western experts on Soviet military expenditures had long suspected.

Shevardnadze wanted the military to be more forthright on verification issues and more candid on data about its defense budget and force levels; senior military officers were determined to hide the real cost of maintaining and equipping their forces. Shevardnadze was a forceful proponent of creating risk reduction and crisis management centers; the military opposed these centers, viewing them as limiting its freedom of action and threatening secrecy.

Divisive Issues

Krasnoyarsk and the ABM Treaty

Shevardnadze's first major challenge to the military occurred in 1986, when he accepted the U.S. position that the Krasnoyarsk phased-array radar station, located deep inside the Soviet Union, violated the ABM treaty prohibiting construction of such radars except on the periphery of the United States or the Soviet Union. The radar did not affect the balance of forces between the two superpowers, according to the U.S. Joint Chiefs of Staff, but the political ramifications of Soviet cheating on the ABM treaty were vast. Many U.S. officials believed that Moscow's deception in building the radar demonstrated that it could not be trusted on any arms control issues; others wanted to use this violation to justify revising the ABM treaty to allow the United States to pursue SDI. Shevardnadze understood the centrality of the ABM treaty to the arms control process and, in his speech at the United Nations in September 1986, recognized that Krasnoyarsk compromised stable deterrence and threatened the integrity of the ABM treaty. He thus signaled the Reagan administration that Krasnoyarsk would be dismantled.

It was left to Shevardnadze to deal with the high-level military and industrial officials in the Defense Council who were reluctant to surrender this important bargaining chip. Although Shevardnadze's criticism of the Krasnoyarsk radar station began in 1986, it was not until 1989 that Gorbachev assured newly elected U.S. President George Bush that Moscow had put an end to Krasnoyarsk "to make things easier for the new president."[54] Shevardnadze told the Supreme Soviet in 1989 that the radar, a "breach of the ABM treaty," had undercut Moscow's efforts to preserve the ABM treaty as the "foundation of strategic stability."[55] He acknowledged that there had been serious opposition to dismantling Krasnoyarsk and added disingenuously that it had taken Moscow four years of "investigation" to determine that Krasnoyarsk was not a satellite tracking station but a sophisticated "battle management" radar in a potential antiballistic missile system.

Arms Control Agreements

Beginning with its declaration of a unilateral nuclear test moratorium in 1985, the new leadership, often led by Shevardnadze, made a series of radical arms control proposals and initiatives that marked a break with the past in Soviet thinking on disarmament and ended the political leadership's previous deference to the military on policymaking. Shevardnadze was responsible for an agreement at the Conference on Disarmament in Europe in 1990, for example, that permitted on-site inspection by third parties of Soviet military activities.[56] The military criticized many of these agreements as one-sided in Washington's favor.

The INF Treaty of 1987 included intrusive and extensive on-site inspections and eliminated all SS-20 intermediate-range missiles in Eurasia. Moscow had to destroy 889 intermediate-range missiles and 957 shorter-range missiles, whereas Washington had to destroy only 846 missiles. Inclusion of the short-range SS-23 in the INF negotiations, which Shevardnadze favored, was strongly resisted by the military.[57]

The Strategic Arms Reduction Talks (START) treaty, signed in July 1991, required ten years of negotiations and led to significant Soviet and American reductions in ballistic missiles. These reductions would take place with the assistance of equipment and technical support from the United States, Britain, Germany, and France, which Shevardnadze would have favored. Washington refused, however, to accept Moscow's efforts to link the signing of the treaty to a commitment of continued

observance of the ABM treaty, a resumption of talks on limiting underground nuclear tests, and the initiation of talks on reducing tactical
nuclear weapons in Europe. This U.S. reluctance increased Shevardnadze's vulnerability to charges that he had sold out to Washington.

Gorbachev and Shevardnadze provided the impetus for the Soviet-
American ban on chemical weapons of 1990. Moscow had not even
acknowledged that it had chemical weapons until 1987, when Gorbachev
declared that the Soviet Union had ended chemical weapons production,
had no chemical weapons outside its own territory, and had begun
construction of a site for their destruction.[58] Shevardnadze indicated that
Moscow would accept the stringent verification principle of "mandatory
challenge inspections without the right of refusal" for facilities suspected
of production or storage of chemical weapons, but the United States
balked at this proposal for intrusive on-site inspection.[59]

In a speech to a foreign ministry conference in 1988, Shevardnadze
bitterly criticized the buildup of chemical weapons, stating that it had
cost a "colossal amount" of money and diverted "production capacities,
manpower, and resources."[60] He charged that the military had done
"major damage" to the Soviet Union's image with these "barbaric"
weapons. In a harsh attack on the military leadership, he called its
rationale for chemical weapons the "most primitive and distorted idea of
what strengthens and what weakens the country." In view of Moscow's
reliance on large ground forces, he said, chemical weapons were far more
dangerous for the USSR than for the United States.

Shevardnadze further angered the military in 1989 with his announcement that Moscow would begin destroying chemical weapons by the
end of the year, yet another unilateral gesture designed to encourage
negotiations with the United States. The signing of the treaty with the
United States in 1990, an otherwise rough year for the foreign ministry
in its battle with the defense ministry, led to a worldwide ban in 1993.

The military resented Shevardnadze's position on chemical weapons
but had to accept their destruction. In addition to the Politburo criticism,
a public campaign charged that these weapons created environmental
damage and health hazards. In 1990 the commander of Soviet chemical
troops established a timetable mandated by the U.S.-Soviet agreement
and promised that safety concerns would be protected. In unusual military
deference to public opinion, the commander promised that, after the
Supreme Soviet chose the sites and plant designs for destruction facilities,
Moscow would "negotiate with the population and local authorities."[61]

Shevardnadze's call for responsible security policy placed the military on the defensive. In addition to the campaign against chemical weapons, groups in the Soviet Union demanded that nuclear test sites on Novaya Zemlya in the Arctic Ocean and Semipalatinsk in Kazakhstan be shut down. The military believed such closings would jeopardize the test program and wanted the United States to join a bilateral nuclear testing moratorium in return for closing the sites. In December 1989, however, the Communist Party in Kazakhstan endorsed public demands for closing Semipalatinsk, and in March 1990 a military official told the Supreme Soviet that the defense ministry planned to transfer all test operations to the Arctic by 1993.[62]

The defense ministry's decision to close down Semipalatinsk meant that, within several months, the military agreed to close down a major nuclear test site without a reciprocal U.S. shutdown, canceled plans for a chemical weapons destruction facility on the Volga River because of local protests, and announced a moratorium on construction of a new ballistic missile early warning radar in Ukraine. Scientists had linked underground nuclear testing at Semipalatinsk, nuclear waste storage near Chelyabinsk in the Urals, and nuclear submarine activity in the White Sea to ecological decay in those areas.

The conclusion of the Conventional Forces in Europe (CFE) Treaty, signed at the CSCE summit in Paris in November 1990, just a month before Shevardnadze's resignation, marked a one-sided Soviet retreat from Central Europe, with Moscow withdrawing 370,000 troops from the region and the United States withdrawing only 60,000. The CFE treaty, calling for a 30 percent reduction in conventional weapons, represented the most ambitious arms control treaty in history and earned Shevardnadze the undying enmity of the Soviet military. An officer with the Southern Group of Forces criticized Shevardnadze for "selling off our national might" and asserted that the foreign minister's "amazing flexibility" in the negotiations "borders on the unscrupulous."[63]

In a defiant act, even before the signing of the agreement, the General Staff had approved the movement of thousands of tanks and artillery pieces beyond the Urals—a violation of the spirit, if not the text, of the treaty. More seriously, Moscow redesignated three motorized rifle divisions as naval infantry units, which were not covered by the treaty. The redesignation was the General Staff's response to a treaty that created much lower levels of conventional arms for the Soviet Union than for NATO. An angry Shevardnadze, caught off guard by the military's action, complained to Gorbachev, who responded that his military adviser, Marshal Akhromeyev, had assured the Politburo that the army had taken no steps that contravened the treaty.[64]

Only several days before Shevardnadze's resignation, *Krasnaya Zvezda* campaigned to stop ratification of the treaty, expressing concern that CFE undermined Soviet security. Following the loss of Eastern Europe, the disintegration of the Warsaw Pact, and German membership in NATO, the military viewed the treaty—particularly the call for immediate destruction of equipment—as the final straw in Shevardnadze's betrayal of Soviet national interests.

The Military Counterattack

In responding to attacks on its institutions and policies, the military focused its criticism on Shevardnadze. Military officials charged that he had instigated media criticism and wrongfully accused the General Staff of exercising a stranglehold over Soviet foreign policy.[65] They scoffed at his call for "democratization of decision-making," stating that he had in fact invited very little discussion of decisions to limit defense spending, procurement, and the use of force.[66] They criticized his concessions to the United States, indicating that he made unilateral concessions that the military had never blessed. In 1990, Yazov and Moiseyev attacked Shevardnadze for cutting defense spending.[67]

Senior military officials blamed Shevardnadze for their loss of influence on national security matters and for undermining dialogue between the foreign and defense ministries by his refusal to consult with them. Ambassador Yuly Vorontsov has stated that Shevardnadze's attitude toward the military was, in fact, dismissive and that if he had attempted to establish a dialogue he might have been more successful.[68] Gorbachev acknowledged that he had to mediate between Shevardnadze and the military, referring to his foreign minister as "the passionate Caucasian" who often "lost his temper with Defense Ministry officials."[69]

Retired Major General Alexander Vladimirov has argued that the military agreed with much of Gorbachev's agenda, including disarmament and even unilateral reductions, but resented Shevardnadze's efforts to circumvent the decision-making process.[70] The absence of any consultation on Gorbachev's speech to the United Nations in December 1988, in which he announced unilateral reductions, effectively ended the dialogue between the defense ministry and the foreign ministry, according to Vladimirov.

The army resented taking the blame for the tragedy in Tbilisi in 1989 and held Shevardnadze responsible for criticism of its role. Over the objections of the General Staff, he had allowed teams of American and French doctors to conduct an independent investigation in Tbilisi, internationalizing the tragedy and embarrassing the military, which deeply resented being blamed for what it viewed as a political problem.[71]

By late 1989, military dissatisfaction had been exacerbated by the loss of the Soviet position in East Germany. The military blamed Shevardnadze for the reunification of Germany in 1990 and the hasty exit of Soviet forces from Eastern Europe. At home, the military had been ravaged, with large defense cuts unmatched by U.S. cuts, while Soviet officers and their families, forced to return from abroad, faced severe housing problems.

The military criticized Shevardnadze, an advocate of the nonuse of force, for Gorbachev's unwillingness to take action in 1989 and 1990 to halt Lithuania's drift toward independence, which threatened military facilities there, especially air defense and lines of communication. The military faced armed insurrections in Armenia and Azerbaijan as well as increased opposition to conscription in the Caucasus and the Baltics. Moiseyev claimed that 1,200 army deserters were hiding in the Caucasus and that many of them had joined armed separatists in Armenia and Azerbaijan.[72] These problems led to deployment of special forces in 1990 in the southern-tier republics.

The net result of military intervention was increased enmity for the military among the people and greater instability within military ranks. Authoritative accounts of waste and corruption within the military as well as the withdrawal from Afghanistan contributed to the demythologizing of the Red Army. By 1990, applications to military academies were down, and military faculties at higher educational institutions were under siege.[73] Greater numbers of the draft-age population were finding ways to avoid military service.

Representatives of the military-industrial complex and the Politburo believed that reductions in defense spending and nuclear capabilities were reducing Moscow's global influence. These hardliners believed (correctly) that Moscow's world role derived solely from its military power and that any reduction in force would limit Soviet political and diplomatic influence.

The promotion of Yazov to Marshal and the staging of a military parade on Victory Day in 1990 marked Gorbachev's shift to the right and Shevardnadze's loss of power. The use of military force in Lithuania and Azerbaijan in 1990, and the military's moves to circumvent CFE, demonstrated Gorbachev's political dependence on the military and Shevardnadze's loss of influence.

The Law of Unintended Consequences

During their five-year partnership, 1985–90, Gorbachev and Shevardnadze diminished the military's influence, significantly reduced the defense budget, entered into extensive arms control agreements with the United States, and staged a major withdrawal of Soviet forces from regions outside Soviet borders. Shevardnadze registered a series of victories over the General Staff, outmaneuvering it on INF, START, a chemical weapons ban, CFE, and unilateral withdrawals. The strategic retreat from Central Europe, the Sino-Soviet border, and the Third World was accomplished, as were the return of the Soviet fleet to its home waters and the dismantling of Soviet bases abroad.

Some of Shevardnadze's victories had unforeseen consequences. Not long after his resignation, the military began to complain that CFE restrictions were affecting its ability to deal with confrontation on its borders. With the dissolution of the Soviet Union, Russia was faced with a series of flash point situations in Central Asia and the Caucasus, but the CFE limited the military's ability to deploy force. Russian officials argued that the treaty's subregional restrictions prevented Moscow's response to the ethnic violence in the Caucasus, particularly Georgia, and pressed for changes in CFE sublimits. Russian military commanders threatened to create new armies in North Caucasus, even if that meant violating the terms of the CFE treaty.[74]

Shevardnadze's campaign against the military eroded the Red Army's power and prestige in Soviet society. His use of glasnost ended the military's monopoly on defense information and fostered a blizzard of criticism of military decisions and practices. The Rust affair in 1987 allowed a purge of the high command; the unilateral withdrawal of Soviet forces in 1988 began a strategic retreat in Central Europe; and the Tbilisi tragedy in 1989 made the military fair game for criticism at every level. Every military step backward led to an advance for Shevardnadze and his foreign ministry.

Ultimately, however, Shevardnadze failed as a diplomat and negotiator in dealing with the defense ministry and the General Staff. Many senior officers supported rapprochement with the West, disarmament, and even significant cuts in strategic forces. Their problems were with unilateral cutbacks and reductions in conventional forces that compromised Moscow's quantitative edge in Central Europe.

The military believed it had to challenge Shevardnadze for his failure to consult fully on sensitive matters and to get so little in return for major concessions from the United States. Unfortunately, Washington contributed to Shevardnadze's demise by pushing the foreign minister to the limit on each and every issue, without realizing the cost in terms of his loss of influence.

The military won the battle against Shevardnadze with his resignation in 1990, but it ultimately lost the war in August 1991, when the coup attempt of the Committee of Eight failed. Defense Minister Yazov's association with the Committee of Eight was a fool's errand, his lack of political acumen further weakening his institution. The military's decline continued with its attack on the Russian White House in October 1993 and its invasion of Chechnya in 1994. Clearly the Red Army had lost its icon status in Russian society.

According to Vorontsov, Shevardnadze never understood the Soviet military's pride in its quantitative superiority over Western forces.[75] The military had not forgotten its defeats in the early years of World War II and relied on superior numbers to prevent future setbacks. It expected compensation for giving up conventional superiority in Central Europe but could never arrange a dialogue with the foreign minister. Akhromeyev told Vorontsov in 1990 that the military would "hang him [Shevardnadze] some day" for giving in to the United States. Subsequent Russian military support for secessionist forces in Georgia in 1993 suggested that a way had been found to do so.

MINIMIZING THE PARTY'S ROLE

Weakening Central Committee Departments

Gorbachev and Shevardnadze recognized that the Communist Party, with its ideological and conservative baggage, was an impediment to the implementation of new thinking. Their strategy was to remove "old thinkers"; weaken the Central Committee departments responsible for security policy; and undermine the authority of the main party organs, the Politburo and the Secretariat.

The first target was the Central Committee's International Department. Boris Ponomarev, the department's chief for twenty-five years, was replaced in 1986 by Shevardnadze's putative rival, Anatoly Dobrynin. Speculation that Dobrynin would bring the U.S. portfolio to the department and challenge Shevardnadze's influence failed to materialize. In 1987, the department was weakened by creation of a new party International Policy Commission, headed by Politburo member Yakovlev, close ally of Gorbachev and Shevardnadze. As chairman of the commission, Yakovlev was responsible for ensuring implementation of decisions on foreign policy.[76] Dobrynin's International Department, forced to report to the commission, lost power and influence.

The Central Committee's Department for Liaison with Communist and Workers' Parties of the Socialist Countries also was weakened, first by the removal of its longtime chief, Konstantin Rusakov, then by its merger (in 1988) with the International Department and the Cadres Abroad Department. This merger effectively ended the special status accorded to the party in relations with socialist countries.

In 1989, Dobrynin was removed as head of the International Department and dropped as party secretary.[77] His senior deputies, Korniyenko and Vadim Zagladin, also were purged, thus eliminating key individuals who opposed Shevardnadze and had career ties to Gromyko. Dobrynin was replaced by Valentin Falin, former director of the Novosti news service.[78] Unlike Dobrynin, Falin supported Shevardnadze on such key issues as East-West relations, the need to reduce military spending, arms control, and the irrelevance of the doctrine of class struggle.[79] However, he and many members of the foreign ministry parted company with Shevardnadze over the issue of German reunification.[80]

A purge of the Central Committee in 1989 eliminated the most powerful individuals remaining in the party, including Gromyko and Vasily Kuznetsov, a relic of the Stalin era and a senior diplomat who had been first deputy chairman of the Presidium of the Supreme Soviet. Stepan Chervonenko, former chief of the Cadres Abroad Department and the ambassador in Czechoslovakia during the Soviet invasion in 1968, also was purged.[81] Nearly one-quarter of the members of the Central Committee lost their positions. Shevardnadze justified these changes as a "democratization" of decision-making, but in fact they helped consolidate decision-making authority in his hands.[82]

Creating Commissions and Councils

Gorbachev created the party's Ideological Commission and International Policy Commission in 1988. Headed by allies Vadim Medvedev and Alexander Yakovlev, these commissions were designed to streamline decisions, ensure innovative thinking, and bypass the Politburo.[83] Central Committee departments now reported to the commissions, not to the Politburo, further weakening the party and strengthening Shevardnadze's role as Gorbachev's most influential adviser on foreign affairs. The commissions themselves held few meetings and contributed little to the policy process. Their main purpose was to diminish the role of existing party organs.

The Defense Council, the senior decision-making group for security problems, was a precursor of the presidential commissions that Gorbachev would create toward the end of his tenure.[84] Dominated by the military and reporting to the Politburo, the council had no independent staff and relied on information provided by the KGB and the General Staff; its members were rarely identified in the press, and virtually nothing was known of their discussions.[85] Under the draft constitution announced in 1988, the president of the Supreme Soviet became chairman of the Defense Council, marking another victory for Shevardnadze in reducing the role of the party and the military in national security policy.

To counter charges that he and Shevardnadze were operating in an authoritarian manner, Gorbachev established a Presidential Council in 1990 to vet foreign policy issues. This moved security decision-making from the Politburo to the office of the president, which was acquiring powers similar to those of a U.S. president. After Shevardnadze's resignation, Gorbachev abolished the Presidential Council and created a Security Council. He emphasized that the Security Council would operate "practically daily" and would "decide all questions of . . . security," including matters of the "economy . . . and interethnic conflict."[86] His appointments to the Security Council reflected his move to the right. The only full-time members, Vadim Bakatin and Yevgeny Primakov, were moderate reformers, but most ex officio members of the council were conservatives: Premier Valentin Pavlov, Vice President Gennady Yanayev, Internal Affairs Minister Boris Pugo, Defense Minister Yazov, and KGB Chief Vladimir Kryuchkov. All of the ex officio members took part in the coup against Gorbachev in 1991.

Neither the Presidential Council of 1990 nor the Security Council of

1991 ever assembled a genuine staff system or became part of the policy process. The failure to use these councils during the crises in the Persian Gulf and the Baltics in 1990–91 reflected their irrelevance. At the same time, the party's Politburo and secretariat also had been shut out of major decisions and rarely met on sensitive policy matters; there were no Politburo meetings during the Persian Gulf and Baltic crises.[87] Gorbachev and Shevardnadze had effectively undermined the party's role in decision-making but had failed to create credible institutions to replace them.

Empowering the Supreme Soviet

Shevardnadze favored a more-prominent foreign affairs role for the Supreme Soviet—the USSR's legislative body that had been a rubber stamp for security policy—perhaps hoping to create the illusion that Moscow was becoming a more democratic society. The power taken from the party secretariat in foreign policy ostensibly was given to the Supreme Soviet, with Shevardnadze persuading Gorbachev to create permanent legislative committees similar to parliamentary groups in Western governments to oversee the conduct of foreign policy. He argued that the mistakes of the Brezhnev era could have been prevented if policy had been debated in the legislature. He sought no debate of his own controversial decisions, however, and resented the Supreme Soviet's intrusions into his territory.

The new permanent committees of the legislature monitored the party's conduct of defense and foreign affairs, held hearings, confirmed ministers of defense and foreign affairs, and passed legislation. They approved budgets of the ministries, which suggested a role in monitoring the defense budget.[88] The Supreme Soviet also received oversight functions on national security, with accountability being introduced at the legislative level for the first time. The commissions helped to erode the military's monopoly over decision-making and reduce secrecy in the policy process.

Supreme Soviet committees for security policy and military affairs—the Committee on Defense and State Security and the Committee for International Affairs—increased the role of the government in decision-making. These were permanent bodies with full-time staffs, modeled after the committee structure of the U.S. Congress, particularly the Foreign Affairs and Foreign Relations Committees of the House of Representatives and Senate, respectively. With limits on staff access to sensitive information, however, it was difficult for them to play a real role in policy formation.

The Supreme Soviet never acquired genuine influence in national security, but it embarrassed Shevardnadze during the Persian Gulf crisis. Only two months before his resignation, Shevardnadze was summoned to the Supreme Soviet to explain his policy on the use of force in the Gulf. Many deputies feared that the use of force would jeopardize the safety of Soviet citizens in Iraq. The Committee for International Affairs also deplored the insufficient security guarantees and financial benefits from Germany as a price for reunification. Shevardnadze defended his need to respond quickly to both events without consulting the legislature, because the fast pace "demanded a very complicated and . . . tough schedule for foreign policy." He warned that "falling behind" could mean losing the "opportunity" to pursue Soviet interests. [89]

A Powerless Party

By 1991 the Communist Party of the Soviet Union had been rendered powerless. For more than seventy years this institution had ruled supreme, ruthlessly dominating the nation through repression and collusion with the Soviet military and the KGB. The party had been in gradual decline since the death of Stalin, but its hold on the Soviet Union's institutional levers and the lack of challenge to its authority enabled it to retain power.

The radical reforms of Gorbachev and Shevardnadze brought down the corrupt and inflated party apparatus. No other institutions, either old or new, were able to pick up the pieces, however, and the result was an institutional power vacuum. Virtually all institutions and all leaders had been thoroughly discredited by 1991, when the Soviet Union fell apart. Fortunately, Gorbachev and Shevardnadze, through their emphasis on the nonuse of force, had helped to prepare the way for a nonviolent demise rather than the bloodbath that might otherwise have ensued.

5

THE CENTRALITY OF
THE UNITED STATES

No matter where we
turned, we came up
against the fact that we
would achieve nothing
without normalization of
Soviet-American relations.
We did some hard thinking,
at times sinking into de-
spair over the impasse.
—Eduard Shevardnadze

In 1917, the Russian Revolution produced a totalitarian state with a
confrontational international policy. In 1985, Gorbachev and Shevardnadze began a second revolution, dismantling Bolshevik controls and
pursuing international reconciliation. The key to the second revolution
was to end both the Cold War and the competition with the United
States. From the outset, Shevardnadze focused his energy and diplomatic
effort on solving the "American problem" in order to gain breathing
space (*peredyshka*) for reviving Moscow's failed economy. A "state needs
order," Shevardnadze said, "especially a state like ours . . . in severe
crisis."[1]

His focus on the United States stood in stark contrast to the limited
attention Shevardnadze gave other countries in his first year as foreign
minister. Western Europe seemed almost nonexistent, and his visionary
talk about the "common European home" was just that—mere talk.

Third World leaders criticized his lack of attention to their problems. Asia was given short shrift, and not even China and Japan were treated as major political and economic states to be courted.

Shevardnadze understood that Soviet-American rivalry in the 1980s was far different from a decade earlier, when Washington was on the defensive. In the 1970s the Soviet Union achieved strategic parity with the United States and gained influence throughout the Third World. In contrast, the United States had withdrawn from Vietnam in disarray and backed away from competition in Africa. A decade later, however, Soviet leaders faced failure in Afghanistan, an assertive Reagan administration, and the introduction of modern U.S. forces on Moscow's southern flank in Southwest Asia. Shevardnadze did not believe the Reagan administration's propaganda about U.S. military weakness and never doubted U.S. military power and determination to resist Soviet expansion.[2]

With his commitment to rapprochement with the United States, Shevardnadze brought to the foreign ministry a willingness to compromise. In his first two years, he offered concessions on issues that he believed would have resonance in Washington, particularly disarmament and human rights, making one gesture after another in his efforts to forge a new relationship. His disproportionate concessions in arms control allowed Washington to get "120 percent of what it wanted in negotiations" with the Kremlin, according to U.S. Ambassador Jack Matlock.[3]

Shevardnadze's compromises on nuclear testing, naval nuclear weapons, and antisatellite weapons attracted no response from the United States. His support for deep reductions in the Soviet arsenal, however, led to disarmament agreements that were overwhelmingly favorable to the United States, particularly the agreement on intermediate-range nuclear forces in 1987 that ended the Soviet buildup in Europe and Asia. If the United States had been more responsive, the large reductions in strategic arms agreed to in 1991 and 1993 (START I and II) could have been negotiated several years earlier.

The key to progress was Shevardnadze's close personal relations with his U.S. counterparts, Secretaries of State Shultz and Baker. He used his innate graciousness and sense of humor to insinuate himself with both men and to leaven the opposition of anti-Soviets in the Reagan and Bush administrations. He used his access to Gorbachev to isolate the anti-Americanists at home.

Every step of the way, the foreign minister met disbelief, skepticism, and astonishment in Washington, which had the most to gain from his willingness to compromise. The United States, which had spent so much treasure countering the Soviet threat, had no idea how decrepit the USSR had become and how great an opportunity was being offered. President Reagan saw the struggle between the United States and the Soviet Union as a struggle between good and evil; his references to the "aggressive impulses of an evil empire" took on a life of their own until Shultz persuaded him that historic agreements could be reached.[4] President George Bush came to office believing that Shultz had been too impressed with Shevardnadze and too eager to improve bilateral relations. Baker, initially skeptical, came to believe that Moscow was genuinely committed to redefining relations and persuaded President Bush to continue negotiations with Moscow.

Because the United States was so slow to respond and offered so little in return for major Soviet concessions, Shevardnadze faced severe criticism at home. He was attacked for making unilateral force reductions and for granting the United States one-sided agreements. His critics linked his willingness to accede to U.S. wishes to the Soviet withdrawal from Eastern Europe and ultimately to the dissolution of the Soviet Union itself. Ironically, Shevardnadze's greatest success, establishing close working relations with Washington and helping to end the Cold War, would become one of the major reasons for his downfall.

Domestic opposition to Moscow's conciliatory approach toward the United States caused Gorbachev to acknowledge that there were "militarist, aggressive forces" in Moscow hoping to "perpetuate confrontation." In 1986, he answered his own rhetorical question: "What, comrades, are we to do? Slam the door?"

> It cannot be ruled out that that is exactly the sort of thing they are pressing us to do. But we are keenly aware of our responsibility for the fate of the country, for the fate of peace. And for this reason we do not intend to play up to those who would want to make humanity grow accustomed to the nuclear threat and the arms race.[5]

The domestic critics of Gorbachev and Shevardnadze demanded reciprocal concessions from Washington. They became more vocal as the anti-Soviet policymakers of the Reagan and Bush administrations resisted Shevardnadze's conciliatory gestures. Senior military officers were distraught over disarmament agreements that ended Moscow's quantitative advantages in strategic and conventional weapons. Conservatives in the Politburo feared that the end of strategic parity with the United States would destroy Moscow's investment in the arms race. Critics in the foreign ministry argued that Shevardnadze's approach had become unbalanced and threatened broader Soviet interests. These critics combined to force Shevardnadze's resignation in 1990.

THE REAGAN ADMINISTRATION

U.S. Resistance to Rapprochement with the USSR

Reagan and Bush were slow to respond to Shevardnadze's efforts to improve Soviet-American relations and accelerate disarmament negotiations. Reagan's national security advisers, particularly Richard Allen, William Clark, and John Poindexter, were anti-Soviet and had little understanding of the politics of arms control. Reagan himself was prepared to meet with Soviet leaders, but these advisers—along with Secretary of Defense Caspar Weinberger and CIA Director William Casey—argued that he should complete the defense buildup and create the foundation for the Strategic Defense Initiative (SDI) before engaging in serious negotiations.[6] Precious time was wasted because of this failure to recognize that the Cold War could be ended.

The Soviets, concerned with U.S. development of antisatellite and antimissile space weaponry and anxious to move toward rapprochement with Washington, wanted a summit meeting as early as the summer of 1985. They advanced a series of unilateral arms control initiatives, signaling their commitment to conciliation. A month after Shevardnadze became foreign minister, Moscow announced the first of three six-month periods of unilateral nuclear test moratoriums. Moscow even allowed the National Resources Defense Council, a private organization, to establish seismic monitoring stations in the Soviet Union in 1986 to monitor the moratorium. During this eighteen-month period, an unresponsive United States tested at least twenty-six nuclear devices; it would be seven years before a slow-moving U.S. Congress pushed a test moratorium on an even more reluctant White House.

Moscow also announced a six-month moratorium on deployment of intermediate-range missiles in Europe, then accepted U.S. terms for removing all intermediate-range missiles from Europe. Shevardnadze personally lobbied in the Kremlin for stringent verification requirements, including on-site inspection. He believed that "arms control without verification was impossible" and accepted Reagan's paraphrase of a Russian proverb: "Trust but verify." By failing to respond constructively to Moscow's unilateral actions, the United States missed an opportunity to support Shevardnadze's challenge to the Soviet military.

Forging Relations with Shultz

Shevardnadze's energy and self-assurance enabled him to develop extremely close relations with Secretary Shultz, who in turn waged a long and intense bureaucratic battle to convince the White House that the Kremlin was genuinely interested in rapprochement. Shultz had major differences with Secretary of Defense Weinberger, CIA Director Casey, National Security Council adviser Poindexter, and Arms Control and Disarmament Agency Director Kenneth Adelman over Soviet-American relations and arms control. Other than first lady Nancy Reagan and Ambassador Matlock at the National Security Council, Shultz had few allies outside the State Department.[7]

Shultz admitted that he had never heard of Shevardnadze when he was named foreign minister in July, but that he liked him before meeting him. He was particularly grateful that he would no longer have to deal with Gromyko.[8] The secretary had asked his ambassador in Moscow, Arthur Hartman, if there wasn't "something better I can do with my life than meet with that son of a bitch?"[9] Discussions between Shultz and Shevardnadze proved to be "free of the stiff dialogue and tension" that had marked negotiations with Gromyko.[10] Shultz described his new counterpart: "Right out of line management, not a staff man. . . . You can see lots of cases where people on the other side read from pieces of paper that somebody gives them, and that's all they have to say. That's not the way he is."[11] Even when they differed on contentious arms control issues, Shevardnadze and Shultz preserved an air of civility in their discussions.

First Meeting in Helsinki

Shevardnadze's first major task as foreign minister was to prepare for his meeting with Shultz in Helsinki in September 1985. The timing was not propitious. Retired Navy Chief Warrant Officer John Walker had been arrested in the spring in what turned out to be a damaging spy case, and the first FBI agent in history was indicted (and later convicted) for espionage. In September, former CIA officer Edward L. Howard defected to Moscow, compromising CIA personnel and operations. Evidence that the KGB was using "spy dust" to track U.S. diplomats in Moscow led to charges that the chemical compound being used was carcinogenic. These allegations proved false, but they contributed to the perception in Moscow that conservative circles in Washington were trying to prevent improvement in Soviet-American relations. Gorbachev told Western interviewers that the United States was waging a "campaign of hatred" against the Soviet Union.[12]

The Helsinki meeting was designed both to prepare for a Reagan-Gorbachev summit in Geneva in November and to mark the tenth anniversary of the Helsinki accords. The accords had ratified existing frontiers in Europe and reaffirmed the principles of sovereign equality of states, inviolability of frontiers, territorial integrity, nonintervention in the internal affairs of other countries, and renunciation of force to change existing frontiers. They also had proclaimed the so-called Basket Three provisions requiring each signatory to guarantee the protection of basic human rights within its borders.

The opening session of the meeting was far from smooth. Although Shultz later praised the absence of polemics at the meetings, he himself delivered a hard-hitting speech on Soviet human rights violations. He firmly believed that the human rights issue had to be a fundamental part of the superpower dialogue and that rights violations had isolated the USSR and contributed to its backwardness.[13] Shultz's comments on human rights did not fall on deaf ears. Georgians had a reputation for tolerance, particularly toward their Jewish minority; Shevardnadze himself had taken political risks in the 1970s to protect minorities in Tbilisi. He would later tell Shultz that he had not forgotten their initial exchange on human rights and had presented the secretary's case to the Politburo. As a result, Moscow began to modify its policies with respect to dissidents and emigration.[14]

The most important result of the Helsinki session was the forging of close relations between Shevardnadze and Shultz. Shevardnadze, seeking an opportunity to end "suspiciously hostile and vengeful" relations between the United States and the Soviet Union, warmed to Shultz after their first firm handshake.[15] He claimed that he softened passages in his statements in order to foster close ties, and he turned his energy and charm to building the personal relationship that would play the leading role in Soviet-American relations for the next three years.

Thomas W. Simons Jr., deputy assistant secretary for European affairs, quickly noticed that the new foreign minister differed from typical Soviet negotiators. He accepted the use of simultaneous translation, which saved time in negotiations, and he was willing to make snap decisions at the negotiating table; he expressed envy at Shultz's freedom to ignore formal talking points.[16] Shevardnadze did not want to speak from notes but was convinced by old foreign ministry hands to do so.[17] This session in Helsinki marked the first and last time that Shevardnadze read from notes in meetings with Shultz; in the future, he would have cards with him but refer to them only when necessary.

Shultz knew that the selection of Shevardnadze had been an unpopular one at senior levels of the foreign ministry. When he asked the Soviet ambassador in Washington, Anatoly Dobrynin, to describe Gromyko's successor, Dobrynin dismissed his new boss as an "agricultural type."[18] It was obvious to Shultz that Dobrynin, a "looming presence" in Helsinki, felt himself to be Shevardnadze's "keeper, his commissar, his bodyguard." Simons also observed that Dobrynin was unhappy with Shevardnadze's performance, disapproving of Shevardnadze's conversational style and the fact that, once the new foreign minister sat down at the bargaining table, his "handlers" could not control him. Shevardnadze clearly resented this situation. Dobrynin would be recalled to Moscow the following year and moved to the Central Committee's International Department, where he became a leading critic of Shevardnadze and his policies.

A Growing Friendship

Shultz was impressed by Shevardnadze's warmth and affability, and he responded in kind. The two brought their families together, visited each other's homes, and did personal favors for family members. Shultz organized a boat trip on the Potomac, sang "Georgia on My Mind" to Shevardnadze, and arranged for the Yale Russian Chorus to sing Georgian folk songs to Shevardnadze's delegation. At one meeting in Moscow, when there was a great deal of tension over security matters at the U.S. Embassy, Shultz had three Russian speakers from the U.S. Embassy staff sing "Georgia on My Mind" to the Shevardnadzes. Shevardnadze loved these gestures, calling them "great" and "respectful," and he responded in kind.[19] He brought Shultz and his wife into the Shevardnadze family circle, a major sign of friendship in Georgian cultural tradition, and he gave Shultz a picture of the Shevardnadze children and grandchildren, which was prominently displayed in Shultz's home in California, a symbol of the permanent friendship the two men had forged.

Opposition to Friendship

Both men faced strong bureaucratic opposition to their developing relationship. Shevardnadze's colleagues at the foreign ministry were opposed to the personal contacts, and Shultz had to battle CIA resistance when he invited Shevardnadze to his home for dinner. Both had continuing battles with their intelligence chiefs, KGB Chief Kryuchkov and CIA Director Casey respectively, as a result of their move toward rapprochement. Shultz came to believe that he was "misled, lied to, and cut out" by the CIA and that Casey had manipulated the CIA's intelligence analysis on the Soviet Union to convince U.S. policymakers that Gorbachev and Shevardnadze were unfit negotiating partners.[20]

Geneva Summit: November 1985

When Reagan and Gorbachev met in Geneva in November 1985, they did not take advantage of the momentum generated at Helsinki, and the summit proved perfunctory and anticlimactic. Gorbachev had used a Politburo meeting in October to get agreement on withdrawal from Afghanistan, but the United States did not pick up Moscow's first hints that it wanted help getting out. Reagan indulged in a harangue over human rights and began his boorish practice of telling tasteless and inappropriate jokes to the Soviet president. The long and bitter disagreement between Moscow and Washington over the U.S. Strategic Defense Initiative dominated the session as Gorbachev bitterly attacked SDI and Reagan adamantly defended it.[21]

The one bright spot in Geneva was that Reagan and Gorbachev

seemed to warm to each other and, despite the impasse on most arms
control issues, established the groundwork for the later agreement on
intermediate-range nuclear forces. Most important, Shultz and Shevardnadze, who would do the heavy lifting in arms control for the next three
years, found they could discuss difficult issues in a straightforward way.
Shultz was impressed by the easy relations that existed between Gorbachev and Shevardnadze, the only member of the Soviet delegation who
did not "truckle to his boss."[22] It was obvious to the secretary that
the source of Shevardnadze's power was his personal and professional
relationship with Gorbachev. He considered Dobrynin and the others
little more than sycophants and ignored them. In his memoirs, Dobrynin
disparaged Shevardnadze's role in Geneva ("Shevardnadze himself was
not very active at the Geneva meeting") and highlighted the efforts of
Korniyenko; six months later, Korniyenko was gone from the foreign ministry.[23]

Political Problems in Washington

The possibility of taking radical steps to improve bilateral relations was
hampered in 1985 by disarray within the Washington policy community.
The reputed stability of policy during the Reagan years is part of the
mythology of the Reagan presidency. No modern presidency had more
national security advisers than Reagan, and few of them had experience
in foreign policy. Even after four years, the NSC adviser was unable to
ameliorate the constant turmoil either between Shultz and Weinberger
or between Shultz and Casey. Weinberger believed (correctly) that NSC
Adviser Robert McFarlane was blocking his access to the president, a
factor that played a role in McFarlane's resignation in 1985.[24]

Differences over SDI

One important issue reflecting the range of opinions within the administration was the question of the Strategic Defense Initiative. The Soviets
considered SDI a destabilizing threat to land-based ICBMs, the main
part of their nuclear arsenal. Gorbachev and Shevardnadze recognized
that Moscow would have to spend considerable resources pursuing a
counter to SDI, directly undermining their commitment to reduce arms
expenditures. They also considered the SDI program part of a U.S. effort

to steal a march on such commercial applications of technology as high-speed computers, miniaturization, and laser technology.

Within the Reagan administration, major differences over SDI reflected major differences with respect to disarmament and broader relations with the Soviet Union. The dilemma with respect to SDI was that proceeding with such a program would violate the terms of the Anti-Ballistic Missile (ABM) Treaty. Reagan himself was committed to SDI, seeing the planned antiballistic missile system both as a protector of U.S. security and as a hedge against Soviet cheating on future agreements. Many members of the administration and Congress, opposed to any arms control agreements with the Soviet Union, were prepared to use SDI as well as allegations of Soviet cheating on arms control agreements to prevent future agreements. Strong advocates of SDI, such as Weinberger, argued correctly that the Soviet construction of the Krasnoyarsk radar system had violated the ABM treaty. He argued that this violation justified U.S. withdrawal from the treaty, which would allow the United States to pursue SDI.

Although built on the scale of the Egyptian pyramids, the Krasnoyarsk radar station had been under construction for several years before it was discovered by U.S. intelligence.[25] Most experts agreed that the radar did not affect the balance of forces between the two powers, but it was nonetheless a violation of the treaty. At the summit meeting in Reykjavik in 1986, Reagan asked Gorbachev, "If you feel so strongly about the ABM treaty, why don't you dismantle the radar you are building at Krasnoyarsk in violation of the treaty?"[26] More than two years later, at a luncheon for the newly elected president, George Bush, Gorbachev said that Moscow had put an end to Krasnoyarsk "to make things easier for the new president."[27] It had taken Shevardnadze that long to effect the change in policy.

National Security Adviser Poindexter wanted to pursue arms control negotiations with Moscow, but he favored reinterpretation of the ABM treaty to allow the development and testing of space-based systems. And Shultz wanted to fund SDI as negotiating leverage against the Soviets but favored continued observance of the ABM treaty. He feared a backlash in the Congress if the administration tried to reinterpret a treaty that had received congressional ratification, a backlash that could end funding for SDI research. Paul Nitze, the leading U.S. arms negotiator and a conservative on arms control policy, believed that SDI would violate the ABM treaty and did not want to see the United States break the treaty.

The Iran-contra Scandal

The Iran-contra scandal was also causing turmoil in Washington. In fact, at the Geneva summit McFarlane informed Reagan and Shultz about the shipments of Hawk antiaircraft missiles from Israeli inventories to Iran. Even before Iran-contra, McFarlane was having problems with Reagan, who was impatient with his aide's difficult personality and excruciatingly detailed briefings.[28] Several weeks after the Geneva summit, McFarlane resigned. This was a relief to many in the U.S. policy community, particularly Weinberger. McFarlane's departure exacerbated Shultz's problems dealing with Soviet-American relations, removing a proponent of arms control; his replacement, John Poindexter, was more hard-line and less flexible.[29]

The Daniloff Affair

Fractious politics in Washington and U.S. air strikes against Libya in April 1986 prevented Shevardnadze and Shultz from meeting again for ten months. When they did meet, in September 1986, they had bitter exchanges over Moscow's arrest of U.S. News & World Report Bureau Chief Nicholas Daniloff, detained shortly after the U.S. arrest of Gennady Zakharov, a low-ranking Soviet spy. It took nearly twelve hours of diplomacy between Shevardnadze and Shultz to resolve the crisis. If the two men had not already established close ties, more protracted negotiations would have been required. But Shevardnadze believed Shultz when the latter guaranteed that a way would be found to release Zakharov. And Shultz believed Shevardnadze's promise that the exchange would lead to the release of additional Soviet dissidents. Few individuals realized how complicated the issue had become.

The U.S. public believed that Daniloff had been arrested arbitrarily by the KGB, but Shultz and the editor of U.S. News, David Gergen, knew that the journalist had acquired "secret" Soviet documents and photographs and passed them to the U.S. State Department.[30] Shultz was furious when he learned that the CIA station had "exposed Daniloff to the KGB," using his name in a contact with a Soviet source and discussing him on an open phone line. His lawyer at the department, Abraham Sofaer, concluded that the CIA "really reamed Daniloff," allowing the Soviets to collect enough information on the journalist to find him guilty in a U.S. court.[31]

Shultz believed that Casey was blocking resolution of the case, hoping to protect his officers from criticism and keep alive an issue that would compromise Soviet-American contacts. Many members of the press suspected CIA mismanagement of the affair but wanted to protect one of their own and did not go public with sensitive details. Shultz agreed to a trade involving Daniloff and Zakharov and was then criticized by journalists who should have known better. William Safire of the *New York Times* charged that the trade and run-up to the summit were "this generation's Yalta."[32] Safire was a political and ideological compatriot of Casey's and shared his intense opposition to Shultz's efforts to improve relations with the Soviet Union.

Following difficult negotiations with Shevardnadze, Shultz announced only twenty-four hours after Daniloff's release that Zakharov would be expelled. The press was prepared to pounce on the obvious "exchange" that the administration previously had denied it would permit. At that point, Shultz left the podium, and the president entered the room to announce that he had accepted Gorbachev's proposal to meet two weeks later in Reykjavik, Iceland, to prepare for a full-scale summit in Washington the following year. No one in the room expected that Reykjavik would become one of the most controversial and misunderstood summits in the postwar period.

Reykjavik Summit: October 1986

Shevardnadze and Shultz agreed that Reykjavik was the most remarkable summit ever held. Because the two sides failed to reach agreement on limiting strategic weapons, the summit was considered a failure at the time. But the talks created the foundation for a series of significant agreements over the next five years and in the long run must be viewed as a major success. Reykjavik did not take that last dramatic step needed to achieve the breakthrough in arms control that Shevardnadze wanted, but the Soviet delegation convinced a skeptical U.S. president and many of his advisers that Moscow was serious about arms control.

The Reykjavik summit came about suddenly. In the wake of the disaster at the Chernobyl nuclear power plant, which led to international criticism of Moscow's efforts to hide the extent of the damage, Shevardnadze wanted to intensify Moscow's dialogue with Washington, including holding experts meetings in Moscow and Washington during August, the traditional vacation month for the Kremlin.[33] In September, Shevardnadze's press spokesman, Gennady Gerasimov, proposed the separate signing of an INF treaty at Reykjavik, thus signaling that the Soviets were prepared to negotiate substantial agreements.

Gorbachev and Shevardnadze had different goals at Reykjavik. Gorbachev, according to his interpreter Pavel Palazchenko, was consumed by the need to head off SDI and wanted to convince international opinion that SDI, opposed by most NATO countries, was blocking START and INF agreements.[34] Shevardnadze, who had to be careful not to upstage his boss,[35] also opposed SDI but was focused on convincing the United States of Moscow's commitment to disarmament.[36] In the end, Gorbachev failed to mount international pressure against the United States with respect to SDI, but Shevardnadze succeeded in convincing Shultz and his key aides that Moscow was serious about eliminating strategic offensive weapons.

The Soviets demonstrated unprecedented flexibility and diplomatic skill at Reykjavik, tabling proposals for 50 percent reductions in strategic weapons and the elimination of intermediate-range nuclear weapons in Europe. Shevardnadze followed up Gerasimov's signal of September with an offer to delink INF from any strategic agreement. The signing of the INF accord a year later, eliminating *all* intermediate-range nuclear weapons in Europe and Asia, demonstrated that Reykjavik had paved the way for comprehensive arms control.

Akhromeyev's Role

The summit highlighted the importance of Marshal Sergey Akhromeyev, who chaired many of the working groups at Reykjavik, an unusual role for a military officer at a summit meeting. The Central Intelligence Agency had told Shultz not to expect a significant military role at Reykjavik, and there were no senior military representatives on the U.S. delegation, a fact that caused resentment within the U.S. military.[37] Not only was the Soviet military well represented but, according to Shultz, Akhromeyev "presented a most reasonable Soviet face."[38] The U.S. delegation developed a great deal of respect for the Soviet marshal.

A fan of James Fenimore Cooper, like many Russians, Akhromeyev referred to himself as the "last of the Mohicans" because he was one of the last Soviets on the General Staff to have taken part in World War II.[39] He was understandably proud of his role as a sergeant during the siege of Leningrad, having spent one year of the siege without going indoors, and he told Shultz that the battle had been the high point of his life. In the 1980s he initially believed that he was part of another opportunity to save his country, and he was committed to negotiating arms control agreements and reducing the Soviet military burden. Eventually, however, he came to believe that Gorbachev's reforms would "tear up everything that I believe in,"[40] and he became a major opponent of conventional cuts. He resigned as chief of the General Staff in 1988 because of his opposition to unilateral troop withdrawal from Central Europe.[41] In August 1991, shortly after the failed coup attempt against Gorbachev, with which he sympathized, he committed suicide.

Like Shevardnadze, Akhromeyev had an easy relationship with Gorbachev, and it appeared to U.S. negotiators that Gorbachev looked to the chief of the General Staff for advice on national security matters. Shevardnadze also relied on Akhromeyev for an understanding of the intricacies of strategic disarmament, and U.S. negotiators acknowledged that the marshal was prepared to make decisions and even concessions.[42] When the two sides were leaving Hofdi House, the headquarters for the talks, Akhromeyev told Nitze, "I hope you will forgive me. I tried. I was not the one who let you down"—a reference to the failure to arrange a 50 percent cut in offensive arms during a five-year period.[43]

Perceived Failure: Significant Breakthrough

No one took the apparent failure of Reykjavik harder than Shevardnadze and Shultz. They were present at the last meeting between Gorbachev and Reagan and immediately understood the danger of having the two most powerful leaders in the world coming to a substantive deadlock over one issue, laboratory testing for SDI. They established eye contact, realizing it was essential to lower the temperature in the room in order for additional meetings to occur. Shultz, the former labor negotiator, suggested that Gorbachev and Reagan review the bidding so that the two sides could create a balance sheet that would record agreements as well as disagreements. Shevardnadze emotionally warned the two presidents that they shared a common destiny and that history would never forgive their differences. He left Hofdi House with tears in his eyes and what he described as the "darkest face" in the crowd.[44] Shultz, who looked worn and exhausted, later confessed that he "took the criticism of Reykjavik seriously."[45]

Reykjavik had, in fact, registered—in the words of Gorbachev—a "kind of intellectual breakthrough."[46] The Soviet-American dialogue would never be the same; the Reagan-Gorbachev, Shultz-Shevardnadze, and Nitze-Akhromeyev relationships had been fundamentally altered. The Reykjavik formula soon led to an agreement for a 50 percent reduction in strategic arms, a ten-year period of nonwithdrawal from the ABM treaty, and an INF treaty. The U.S. media, preoccupied with the gloom that surrounded that last session of talks at Hofdi House, failed to recognize that the two sides had come close to an agreement to eliminate all strategic nuclear weapons.

The NATO allies and U.S. Joint Chiefs of Staff (JCS) were shocked, moreover, by Reagan's willingness to give up nuclear deterrence without advance consultation and reacted bitterly to the idea of substantial cuts in the nuclear arsenal. Even supporters of arms control in the United States and Western Europe were alarmed by what seemed to be a go-for-broke rush to eliminate American and Soviet offensive strategic weapons. The Chief of the JCS, Admiral William Crowe, was particularly angry with Reagan's proposal to eliminate all ballistic missiles before the turn of the century, a concept the joint chiefs had not been allowed to study. The U.S. military also was annoyed that Akhromeyev was in Reykjavik as the representative of the Soviet military, while a mere staff officer represented the U.S. uniformed chiefs. Just as Moscow had to placate its chief of the General Staff at Reykjavik, Reagan's appointment of General Colin Powell as national security adviser in 1987 was designed in part to pacify military critics of the administration on disarmament.

Reykjavik's Legacy

Reykjavik set a foundation for later success. Reagan had signaled that he was serious about negotiations on nuclear arms. Gorbachev had established that he was Reagan's equal and committed to arms control. Several weeks after Reykjavik, despite the revelation that the United States had been secretly funding contra operations in Nicaragua, Shevardnadze told the press that Moscow would continue to pursue its disarmament agenda. He also expressed increased Soviet flexibility with respect to SDI, indicating that Moscow would agree to the development of prototype American space weapons as part of a comprehensive arms control treaty as long as the models were not tested in space. This opened the door